KRAUSS
ESTABLISHED 1903

KRAUSS

The New Orleans Value Store

Edward J. Branley

The History Press

Published by The History Press
Charleston, SC
www.historypress.net

Page 1: Metal sign at the front door of 1201 Canal Street. *Author photo.*

First published 2017

Manufactured in the United States

ISBN 9781625858627

Library of Congress Control Number: 2017940959

Contents

Acknowledgements

Thanks to Amanda Irle, acquisitions editor at The History Press, for shepherding me through the THP process. Special thanks to the indomitable Dara Rochlin (@BookDoctorDara) for her editing and research skills. Much love to Jennifer Duplantis, Susan Kagan, Christine Stephens, Susan Vollenweider, Melissa Case, Lisa Graves and Tricia Cohen, who all keep me upbeat and smiling. A UNO-alumni tip of the hat and thanks to the staff at the Earl K. Long Library, University of New Orleans, especially James Hodges of the Louisiana and Special Collections section. UNO's library is the repository for the Krauss Collection, and James was wonderful about putting up with my requests for stuff that was up on the fourth floor while the section was in its temporary second-floor abode. Thanks to everyone in the Krauss community of former employees and shoppers who shared wonderful memories and gave me a feel for aspects of the store I didn't know about. I am very grateful to Hugo Kahn, the last president of Krauss Co. Inc., for meeting with me and sharing some of his memories of the store. A hearty BMHS Crusader wave to Ryan Bordenave, whose expertise on Canal Street and the CBD was invaluable. Thanks to Drew Walsh, James Karst, J.D. Thomas, Carlos "Froggy" May and the other denizens of the various New Orleans–related Facebook groups who contributed tidbits and ideas along the way. Thank you, Cait Gladdow and Mark Samuels for your help with the research process. I raise my glass to Chuck Taggart in thanks for his red beans and rice recipe. Hugs and love to all my friends who supported the project.

Acknowledgements

All my love to my wife, Helen, and our boys, Kevin and Lieutenant Justin Branley, USN, who are both too young to have shopped at Krauss but patiently let me tell them about the store. Thanks to all my teachers, as well as all the librarians and archivists whose hard work over the years makes writing a book like this much simpler now. Heartfelt thanks to all the folks at Wakin' Bakin' on Banks Street in Mid-City. I'm very appreciative that Conrad and Zak didn't charge me rent, since 90 percent of the book was written in their wonderful breakfast place.

1
Gumbo

Gris-Gris Gumbo Ya-Ya
—Mac Rebennack, aka Dr. John, "The Night Tripper"

Gumbo is a wonderful soup that combines many flavors and ingredients, turning them into a unique dish that is revered in New Orleans. It's the perfect food analogy to the city of New Orleans itself. And a food analogy is the perfect way to describe New Orleans in the first place.

Gumbo has as many variations as there are cooks who make the soup: Chicken-and-sausage gumbo. Seafood gumbo. Okra. Filé. Oysters. Crawfish? "Not in my gumbo," a chef I know says. Turkey gumbo, made on the day after Thanksgiving. Each one is unique. Each one makes up the big picture.

New Orleans isn't just one big pot of gumbo. The city is a collection of pots. Downtown gumbos include the French Quarter, the Treme, along Bayou St. John, the Sixth Ward and many other neighborhoods. Uptown gumbo is the Central Business District (CBD), the Warehouse District, the Garden District, Faubourg Bouligny, the University District, Carrollton. Back-of-town gumbos exist on both sides of Canal Street. Then there's Canal Street itself. The 140-foot-wide main street isn't merely a dividing line but rather a gumbo in and of itself.

At midnight in the Quarter to noon in Thibodaux, I will play for gumbo
—Jimmy Buffett, "I Will Play For Gumbo"

Like gumbo recipes, New Orleans has changed over time. At the start of the twentieth century, the city was the second-largest port in the United States. It was a city adjusting to twenty years of unprecedented expansion after the Civil War. Immigrants from all over Europe, but particularly from Italy and Germany, made their way to New Orleans at the end of the nineteenth century, shifting the flavors of the gumbos that are the city's neighborhoods.

When the Americans took over New Orleans in 1803, they didn't really bring a gumbo recipe with them. The Anglo Irish brought their own flavors, though, and those blended into the recipes that were already simmering on the stoves. By the 1850s, residents of the city could taste many variations of gumbo, and their reports of how wonderful this was attracted even more people to the magic.

While New Orleans was very much caught up in the political conflicts of the late 1850s that led to the formation of the Confederate States of

Steamboats moored along the Mississippi River at New Orleans. *Library of Congress.*

America, New Orleans recognized that the port was paramount. When it was clear that the blockade of the port by the Union navy was killing the city, Farragut's invasion from the mouth of the Mississippi in April 1862 was a force that locals could not withstand. Union occupation spared New Orleans the fate of Atlanta and enabled the port to continue to grow. Reconstruction allowed the merchants operating shops and stores on Canal Street to re-stock and expand. By the 1880s, dry goods stores supplied a number of ingredients needed to keep the gumbos simmering.

The 1890s brought a huge change to the retail landscape of New Orleans. S.J. Shwartz, financed by his father-in-law, Isidore Newman, opened the first department store in the city, Maison Blanche, in 1895. This development inspired other New Orleans merchants to follow suit, and in 1903, the Krauss brothers shifted focus from niche-market sales to the general-merchandise model. The gumbo pots of 1903 were flavorful and diverse.

Take the French Quarter, the city's first neighborhood. When Adrien de Pauger laid out the plan for the original city in 1725, New Orleans was a French city. The French influence dominated until control of the city was passed to the Spanish in 1766, lest it become one of the spoils of war between the French and the British. The Spanish tweaked the gumbo recipe for twenty years, and then they were forced to totally re-create the recipe after the Great Fire of 1788. French-built homes and buildings were replaced with new ones that followed strict building codes. Spanish Colonial architectural influences left us with the high-walled houses focused on central courtyards, their beauty hidden from passersby on the streets. French priests tending their flock found themselves under the administration of Spanish bishops sent from Havana. The mix of languages, colors and political passions in the port appeared impossible to navigate, but the cooks blended the various ingredients into their gumbos.

The Vieux Carré, the Old Square, dating back to the 1720s, was a vibrant residential neighborhood at the beginning of the twentieth century. The original residents of the French Quarter—the French-Spanish "Creoles"—were the establishment families who didn't want to associate with newcomers. Germans didn't speak much English when they came to New Orleans. Sicilians didn't either, and the Anglo Irish Americans, as well as the Creoles, viewed them as no better than African Americans. The easy solution for the Creoles was to move uptown. As they moved, others filled the gumbo pot. By the time department stores came onto the scene, Italian grocers and bakers, German butchers and African Americans were

Milk wagon in the French Quarter. *Library of Congress.*

the people walking up Bourbon and Royal Streets to those big stores on Canal Street.

New Orleans outgrew the French Quarter by the time of the Louisiana Purchase. Bernard Mandeville de Marigny, son of a wealthy plantation family, decided to get out of the agriculture business. He subdivided his plantation, located on the downriver side of Esplanade Avenue and the French Quarter, into modern-style residential lots. Creoles, African Americans and Germans jumped on those lots and built out the neighborhood. As those first families acquired wealth and influence, many of them left Faubourg Marigny for Uptown. By the time the Krauss brothers opened their store, the flavor of the Marigny gumbo was distinctly Italian.

Like the French Quarter, New Orleans outgrew the Marigny, as immigrants from Europe came to the city in large numbers after the Civil War. The Italian families working in the Quarter and the Germans working along the Riverfront in the Marigny moved farther down the river. The political designation for the neighborhood was the "Ninth Ward," and that name stuck. These immigrants hopped on the Desire streetcar line to join

Old Absinthe House, Bourbon Street, 1905. *Library of Congress.*

the residents of the Quarter as they all went to Canal Street to shop. The Ninth Ward gumbo was a true mix of cultures, until white flight of the 1960s removed much of the Italian and German influence, leaving the neighborhood as predominantly an African American gumbo.

While New Orleans' expansion was primarily up- and downriver, there was movement north, along the navigation canals and Bayou St. John. The Carondelet Canal connected Faubourg Treme from 1795 until the 1920s. That water path to the outside world attracted folks who wanted to live along it. The neighborhood expanded east, from the banks of the bayou. The streets of the French Quarter, which had already been extended north through Treme, now continued, as they met up with Esplanade Avenue.

This northern expansion was typical, following a suburban expansion model. Families who couldn't afford the courtyards of the French Quarter went north, to Treme. Those looking for bigger lots on which to build bigger houses kept going, following the bayou. When they got there, they built homes with front lawns in the English style. Their homes kept distinct French-Spanish features, though, such as wrought-iron fencing. The size of homes near the bayou ran from comfortable two-stories to the grandeur of

The Peristyle in New Orleans City Park in the Mid-City neighborhood, built in 1915. *Library of Congress.*

the Luling Mansion. As the neighborhood matured, less expensive houses popped up in its interior, shotgun doubles and Creole cottages, for blue-collar families.

Faubourg St. John's gumbo was an incredibly diverse mix. Waterfront businesses lined the bayou. St. Louis Cemetery No. 3, at the bayou end of Esplanade Avenue, along with the horse racetrack next to it, gave New Orleans City Railroad Company incentive to run streetcars from the river to the bayou, along Esplanade Avenue. That long run connected with cross-town transit lines as well. Good public transit attracts all types of people to a neighborhood, and that was the case with the bayou. When Krauss Department Store opened, residents of the bayou neighborhood could get into downtown by "riding the belt"—taking the Esplanade and Canal Streetcar lines into town and back home again, as they ran a circular route in opposite directions.

The popularity of Faubourg St. John continued, and folks looking for affordable housing moved even farther north, into Gentilly. Gentilly Road and Grande Route St. John brought streetcars and other vehicles east from the bayou, cemetery and racetrack until they connected with the Pontchartrain Railroad. The trains ran from Faubourg Marigny, out to Lake Pontchartrain, on Elysian Fields Avenue. The high ground of the Gentilly Ridge attracted homeowners, and a new neighborhood grew out from the ridge. The gumbo of Gentilly was less a mix of specific ethnic groups but a true New Orleans flavor, as younger generations of families who had lived in the city for some time moved out of mom and dad's house in the Ninth Ward, looking to establish themselves.

It wouldn't be until after World War II that retail stores expanded into Gentilly. As Krauss sought customers in the early twentieth century, the people of Gentilly made their way to Canal Street, along with everyone else.

The expansion of New Orleans along the Mississippi River ran in both directions from Canal Street. As the Creole families grew out from the Quarter, east and north, the Anglo Irish and Americans who came to the city in the wake of the Louisiana Purchase established themselves on the upriver/uptown side of Canal. The offices and businesses set up by these folks wanted to be close to the main street of the city and the downriver growth. Unwilling to allow the Creoles to control water-borne commerce, the Americans built a second canal, whose turning basin was located along South Rampart Street. This New Basin Canal extended out to the city's West End. Stores and offices replaced homes in those first blocks just past Canal Street, as those who worked in what became known as the Central Business District, or CBD, moved farther uptown.

These offices and stores intersected with the activities of the riverfront within a few blocks of Canal Street. Wharves along the river gave way to warehouses a block or two in, along with light industrial sites. The Germans and Irish who came to New Orleans as human ballast on merchant ships out of Liverpool could find work along the river, so they built houses within walking distance of those jobs. The Irish built their first church parish, St. Patrick's, on Camp Street in 1834. The Irish prayed for the men their families lost to accidents and disease during the construction of the New Basin Canal. Mothers worked hard, praying regularly that their children would fare better in America than their husbands. For the most part, they did, and the Irish community continued to grow, moving farther upriver. By the 1850s, they occupied so much of the riverfront neighborhoods that this section of the city became known as the Irish Channel.

The Irish were not the only ethnic group working along the river. By the 1850s, the Germans, along with Creole families, also made their homes

Above: West End was a popular day-trip destination for New Orleanians to beat the summer heat. *Library of Congress.*

Left: The Hotel Denechaud, on Poydras Street, was considered at the "back" of the Central Business District in 1910. *Library of Congress.*

uptown. The Irish Channel was actually three gumbo pots. The Germans and Irish were so separated, they even built their own cathedral-sized churches, across from each other, on Constance Street. These communities were quite insular, but they still made their way from the Channel back down to Canal Street. When Krauss opened in 1903, the Irish Channel still reflected the divisions on which it was built.

Like Bernard Mandeville de Marigny, plantation owners subdivided the land just upriver from the city, as it was more profitable to build houses than grow cotton and sugar cane. While the Irish Channel grew directly along the river, Americans built luxurious homes in the English style, north of Magazine Street, between Jackson, Louisiana and St. Charles Avenues. By the Civil War, this Garden District was the wealthiest neighborhood in the city outside of the French Quarter. The plantations that remained after the Civil War were subdivided, as uptown now extended from the Garden District, upriver to the former city of Carrollton. As the expansion continued, the streets running up- and downriver were extended: Tchoupitoulas and Annunciation Streets, near the river; Magazine Street, the de facto boundary between rich and poor; and St. Charles Avenue, Freret Street and Claiborne

St. Charles Avenue, Uptown. The St. Charles streetcar line is the oldest continuously operating streetcar line (since 1834) in the United States. *Library of Congress.*

Avenue. Streetcars have operated on St. Charles Avenue since 1834; by the end of the Civil War, street rail crisscrossed uptown.

The uptown pots of gumbo were as unique as the subdivisions created there. The Irish Channel had its deep ethnic divisions. The Garden District's wealth made it difficult for people other than the Anglo Irish, along with a few Creoles, to move in.

Faubourg Bouligny, the subdivision that grew out of the breakup of the Bouligny plantation, extended uptown past the Garden District. Once a hotbed of horse breeding and racing, the area continued the trend of offering land where families could build both small shotguns and larger single-family homes.

Jefferson City and the University District all were more "American" than specific ethnic enclaves, always with the African American flavors blending in to make them interesting.

Even though the city grew upriver, the flow of retail goods did not follow the people. That meant all those families living uptown still had to make their way to Canal Street. Transit operators recognized this, as streetcars snaked their way through the uptown gumbo pots. Buses made connections to the streetcars, so even the folks of Carrollton could shop in the CBD.

As the river wound its way north from the French Quarter, small towns popped up in between the plantations. New Orleans annexed the city of Lafayette early on, absorbing the wealth of the Garden District. Jefferson City, just upriver from Faubourg Bouligny, was next, followed by the city of Carrollton.

By the 1890s, higher education had come to uptown. The Society of Jesus purchased a parcel of land that had been part of the Foucher Plantation. The Jesuits established Loyola University of New Orleans on that site. The Tulane Education Foundation acquired the land next to Loyola, constructing the first buildings of Tulane University in 1904. Both universities designed their campuses so their fronts were along St. Charles Avenue, making both schools easily accessible by streetcar.

With the annexation of the city of Carrollton, the city of New Orleans had pushed expansion as far upriver as the adjoining parish of Jefferson would allow. Carrollton became the northernmost riverfront neighborhood. It was a rich and diverse pot of gumbo, attracting Sicilian farmers from farther upriver into an area already populated by all the different types of folks found in other parts of the city. New Orleans's boundaries along the river were firmly set by the time the Krauss brothers opened shop in the 1200 block of Canal Street.

St. Augustine Catholic Church was the nexus of Treme's Creole community in antebellum New Orleans. *Carlos "Froggy" May.*

Throughout this brief survey of the neighborhoods of New Orleans, note that there isn't a separate black neighborhood. Since the founding of the city, black folks have been ubiquitous, both as slaves and as free people of color. The plantations along the river had significant slave populations, and the planters who maintained homes in the city proper staffed their households with slaves.

Africans did not come to New Orleans exclusively as enslaved humans. The port attracted free men of all colors who were looking to make a living and improve their position in society. Affairs between white masters and their slaves were commonplace. Some masters granted the children of their concubines their freedom. Those folks, along with blacks from the islands, made their homes in New Orleans, initially in Faubourgs Treme and Marigny. By the Civil War, Treme had become the cultural center of the black Creole community. St. Augustine Parish, founded in 1842, was the first truly integrated Christian congregation in the city.

Treme was the nexus, and black folks expanded their influence from there. Bernard Mandeville de Marigny did not segregate sales of lots when he subdivided his land, so the black population of the two neighborhoods adjacent to the French Quarter enjoyed solid growth. That growth continued as the city pushed north, into Faubourg St. John and the Sixth and Seventh Wards. Over time, black Creole evolved into just Creole, as the African American community began to dominate the "downtown back of town" neighborhoods.

The arrest of Homer Plessy as he attempted to ride in a whites-only train car from New Orleans to Covington in 1892 led to the Supreme Court decision *Plessy v. Ferguson* in 1896. That ruling established the constitutionality of separate but equal doctrine and ushered in the Jim Crow era. With the rights of African Americans severely limited in southern states, the Great Migration of African Americans from South to North began. This changed the gumbo of Treme radically. The pot lost a lot of its African American flavor and gained a distinct Sicilian makeup. Still, as Krauss opened, Treme, along with the back of the Central Business District, had a significant black population. That was important in the marketing strategy of the Krauss brothers.

Not all African Americans desired or could afford to just pull up roots and move away from New Orleans. Those who remained lived all across the city, some owning their own homes, others renting housing from whites. Public housing projects constructed during the Great Depression in the 1930s became available to black families after World War II, as the white families got back on their feet, moving into the newer neighborhoods of Mid-City and Lakeview and into the suburbs.

As Sicilians came in numbers to New Orleans in the 1880s and 1890s, they quickly filled up the French Quarter and downriver neighborhoods. When black families sold their homes in Treme, leaving town for good, the Sicilians gladly snapped them up. By the start of the twentieth century, the Italian community in New Orleans was well rooted in the Quarter and Treme (in the section of the neighborhood east of the Carondelet Canal). By 1915, the Italians had moved toward the lake to the point where they petitioned the archbishop to establish a new Catholic parish at the northern end of Canal Street. St. Anthony of Padua became the third Italian church in New Orleans, and the Mid-City neighborhood's gumbo had a clear Italian flavor. Mid-City grew out on either side of Canal Street, from Greenwood Cemetery down to Broad Street, the northern boundary of Faubourg Treme. Light industry along the New Basin Canal and the west bank of Bayou St. John bracketed Mid-City, creating opportunities for the residents. Getting back to town to shop was easy, since Canal Street was just a short walk away.

The Lakeview neighborhood grew from both ends to the middle. The West End and Spanish Fort streetcar lines brought New Orleans out to the lakefront for day trips, as families did what they could to escape the

Battle of New Orleans Monument at Chalmette Battlefield in St. Bernard Parish, 1915. *Library of Congress.*

summer heat. Homes and businesses popped up along the New Basin Canal throughout the early 1900s. In the 1920s, the Orleans Levee Board began extensive land reclamation projects that pushed the south bank of Lake Pontchartrain out and created new subdivisions. Numerous federal projects during the Great Depression brought road and infrastructure improvements to the area.

By World War II, Lakeview's open land gave wartime industry and support a place. Higgins Industries landing craft and patrol boats were cranked out of factories in Lakeview, and the workers in those factories began to move closer to work instead of taking the long streetcar trip on the West End line. After the war, many men took advantage of the benefits of the G.I. Bill to start families in Lakeview.

Streetcars were on the decline after World War II, but the residents of Lakeview were able to get back to downtown via bus, riding down West End and Canal Boulevards to the cemeteries at the foot of Canal Street. From there, they connected to the Canal streetcar line to get to Krauss and the other stores.

Small communities existed outside the city limits for generations, but post–World War II expansion drew folks from the city to Jefferson and St. Bernard Parishes in numbers. School desegregation in the 1950s, coupled with the Civil Rights Act of 1964, created the white flight trend of the time. The early 1960s was the beginning of the suburban shopping mall, but it would be another decade before the trend was so rooted that older folks living in Metairie (Jefferson Parish) and Chalmette (St. Bernard Parish) felt like they didn't have to go to Canal Street to do their shopping.

The Krauss brothers and their employees at 1201 Canal started cooking their own pot of gumbo in 1903. Their recipe changed only slightly in the ninety-four-year life of the store. It was all about taking care of New Orleans.

2

Shopping on Canal

They tell me Canal Street,
Is the longest street in town.
—John Lee Hooker, "Canal Street Blues"

Every city and town has a Main Street, a High Street, a place where everyone converges to do business and shopping. In New Orleans, that thoroughfare is Canal Street.

There really was a canal planned for Canal Street. That's why the boulevard that is now the main street of New Orleans is so wide, 141 feet. The original French plan for the streets of New Orleans was the grid that we now call the Vieux Carré, the Old Square, the French Quarter. The French looked at that western boundary and thought it would be the perfect place to connect the end of Bayou St. John with the Mississippi River. As the British colonies in North America grew, Anglo Irish settlers came down to New Orleans, in addition to the continual influx of French, Spanish and Afro Caribbean folks. Culturally, the two groups were oil and water, and Canal Street was the perfect way to separate them. The wide street became a neutral ground between the two communities. To this day, locals refer to the green space on any wide street in New Orleans as a neutral ground rather than a median. The notion of this boundary being neutral space is more than just a figure of speech. The two communities competed in more ways than one.

Basin Street got its name from the turning basin of the Carondelet Canal, the first connecting Bayou St. John to downtown. *Library of Congress.*

The canal planned for Canal Street was built, but it was deeper into the Creole neighborhood. The Carondelet Canal was completed in 1795. The purpose of the canal was to connect the old portage, the end of Bayou St. John, with the Vieux Carré. Its terminus was a turning basin just outside the French Quarter, one block north of Rampart Street and five blocks downriver from Canal Street. This location gave the older, established families and businesses of the city more control over commerce. The location didn't come about solely because of this, however. By the end of the 1700s, Canal Street had taken on a new role. It was no longer the boundary. It was the High Street.

Two divided communities, French Spanish Creole and Anglo Irish American, would, at face value, create a serious divide in terms of business and commerce in New Orleans. It took a third group to bridge the gap, the Jewish community. Jewish merchants discovered quickly that many on both sides of this divide weren't interested in crossover commerce. Men like Judah Touro recognized this and began to buy property along Canal Street.

Beginning in the 1840s, the land along the city's main street was controlled in large part by Jewish merchants. Canal Street became a literal neutral ground where everyone came to shop.

New Orleans was America's "Second City" for much of the nineteenth century. New York was the largest city in terms of population and tonnage moving in and out of its port, with New Orleans coming next. Ships on coastal runs would make the two cities their start and end points, and trade coming from Spain and its colonies in the New World used New Orleans as the port of entry to North America. It was fitting that New Orleans have a magnificent High Street to impress visitors. Multistory residential buildings with retail space began appearing on Canal Street in the 1830s, along with Christ Church Episcopal, on the corner of Bourbon and Canal, in 1833. The city came together on Canal.

The Vieux Carré is only thirteen blocks wide, and it's about twenty-five blocks from Canal Street down through Faubourg Marigny to the Bywater. As the city grew upriver from Canal, the distances back to the High Street increased. By the 1830s, businessmen had seen an opportunity and constructed a railroad connection between the city of Carrollton (now the

Known as the Place d'Armes when New Orleans was a French colony, Jackson Square is one of the most visible public parks in the city. *Library of Congress.*

"Riverbend" section of Uptown) and Canal Street. The 1830s version of the New Orleans & Carrollton Railroad (NO&CRR) used steam engines, but the noise and smoke annoyed residents of Uptown to the point where the company switched to mule-drawn streetcars and trams. Residents of Carrollton, Jefferson City and Lafayette could walk up to Naiads Street (the name of St. Charles Avenue west of Tivoli Square) and ride bobtail cars into the business district. The NO&CRR expanded operations, crisscrossing Uptown with street rail lines, all with the goal of bringing people to the stores and churches.

Tension and turmoil between North and South in the United States existed in New Orleans in the 1850s, but the hustle and bustle of the port kept the city focused. New Orleanians, from the plantation owners and wealthy businessmen down to the day laborers working the wharves along the river, knew that war would close the port, and that would be bad for everyone. Still, the planters whose slaves worked the land upriver from the city controlled state government, and they were as upset with the election of Abraham Lincoln in 1860 as the rest of the South. The merchants and immigrants of the city began to prepare for a blockade of the port and hard times.

Canal Street did not want to contemplate the possibility of war. The city continued to grow throughout the 1850s. By 1860, transit entrepreneurs had identified a new opportunity: connecting the neighborhoods north of the Vieux Carré and Faubourg Ste. Marie (the Central Business District). The New Orleans City Railroad Company (NOCRR) was incorporated. The company built facilities on Canal and North White Streets, just north of Faubourg Treme. Its first operations on Canal Street ran from this station, to Rampart Street. The NOCRR received the same complaints about the steam trains and switched to mule-drawn streetcars so they could continue the line down to the river. The wide neutral ground of Canal Street was no longer a pedestrian esplanade but a transit hub. The railroad company took pains to maintain the aesthetics of antebellum times, planting trees on either side of the tracks.

The NOCRR board of directors aspired beyond Canal Street. They soon expanded their operations, running streetcars on Esplanade Avenue and Rampart Street/St. Claude Avenue. These lines connected the downtown back of town neighborhoods of Faubourg Treme and Faubourg St. John with Canal Street.

It was difficult for merchants with their eyes on Canal Street to capitalize on these streetcar lines, as the State of Louisiana joined the rest of the South

Streetcars at Canal and Rampart Streets, the transit hub one block from Krauss. *Library of Congress.*

in seceding from the Union in 1861. The Union navy established a blockade of the port that remained for a year and a half. Flag officer David Farragut, along with sailors and marines of his squadron, occupied the city on April 28, 1862. This was a devastating blow to the hopes of the Confederacy but quite the relief to New Orleans, as Union control meant the port would come back to life. The city rode out the war under Union occupation, sparing it the fate of other Confederate cities such as Natchez, Mississippi, and Atlanta, Georgia. Canal Street was not bombed; it did not burn. People came to shop, mostly by streetcar.

Putting the United States back together after the Civil War was a painful process in many ways. The dark side of Reconstruction came to New Orleans in the 1870s, but it was soon overwhelmed, as immigrants from Europe came to the city in large numbers, seeking new opportunities. The Vieux Carré became less of a French Quarter, as Sicilians opened groceries, bakeries and pasta factories within its confines. German immigration to New Orleans continued after the war. The population of the city began to grow rapidly, further cementing its position of importance in the country.

Canal Street, from Basin Street, looking toward the river, 1930. *Library of Congress.*

This growth was recognized by the city's merchants. More dry goods stores appeared on Canal Street. The Shwartz family, led by patriarch Abram, had A.J. Shwartz & Sons. When his store burned in 1894, Abram's son, Simon, opened S.J. Shwartz & Company, down the street at the corner of Canal and Dauphine. Backed by his father-in-law, Isidore Newman, he expanded his dry goods store into Maison Blanche, a full department store, in 1897.

And the streetcars brought people from all over town to Canal Street to shop. Electricity came to the transit system in New Orleans in 1894, when the St. Charles line retired its mules. The Canal Street line followed a year later. By 1920, there were over 225 miles of streetcar tracks in New Orleans and interurban rail connections to Kenner and Milneburg.

Canal Street stores and shops first opened in the blocks closest to the Mississippi River. By the 1880s, the street was full of multistory buildings housing retail on the first and second floors, with offices and apartments on higher floors. The growth slowed down at the end of the French Quarter. By the time Canal reached Rampart and Basin Streets, residential replaced commercial. This became the upper boundary of the Central Business District.

There were several reasons for this boundary. On the downtown side of Canal Street, Basin Street was the location of the turning basin for the Carondelet Canal. The corner of Canal and Basin Streets was also the terminus for steam trains going out to the Spanish Fort resort/entertainment complex on Lake Pontchartrain. On the Uptown side of Canal, the New Basin Canal's turning basin was on South Rampart Street. The New Basin Canal, which was eclipsing the older Carondelet Canal, drew the railroads to it, creating a commercial district on that side of Canal Street.

There were ample opportunities for merchants and entrepreneurs in the 1890s and early 1900s. Railroads connected New Orleans and its port to the rest of the continent. Goods came up the river from other countries as cotton went out. The same railroads carried people short distances, to Jackson, Mississippi; Mobile, Alabama; and the Florida Gulf Coast. Trains consisting of green Pullman sleeping cars carried passengers from Los Angeles, Chicago, Boston, New York—and many cities along the way—to New Orleans. In the 1890s, those trains began and ended their New Orleans journeys at Union Station, near the New Basin Canal on South Rampart Street and the Louisville and Nashville station at the head of Canal Street, by the river. Both stations were a short walk or streetcar ride to the stores. This flipped the notion of the day trip on its head. Instead of New Orleanians hopping on trains to escape the city heat, folks who were a two- to four-hour train ride away would come down for the shopping.

More customers meant more opportunities, which meant more merchants looking to set up shop.

The Illinois Central, Union Pacific and Southern Pacific railroads approached the city from the north and west; the Southern and Louisville

Canal Street at night, 1910. *New Orleans Public Library.*

and Nashville from the north and east; and the Gulf, Mobile and Ohio from the Gulf Coast. The trains bracketed Canal Street for roughly the length of the original Vieux Carré, Rampart, to the river. A shopper riding streetcars from Uptown could get off at Carondelet and Canal Streets and walk up or down Canal to their favorite stores, but things were more complicated for rail travelers. They had luggage to contend with, and walking from Rampart up to Carondelet or Magazine was a major challenge. The various street rail operators in the 1890s (consolidation into a single entity would not happen for another ten years) recognized this. The "Canal Street Zone" evolved. Canal Street became a four-track system. Lines coming from Uptown and Downtown would turn on Canal from an intersecting street, travel on the outer track for a block, then turn back onto another cross street for their outbound runs. To reduce the number of transfers in the zone, streetcar lines that came to Canal from streets closer to the river would head outbound (away from the river, towards the lake) Canal, to Rampart Street. This transit configuration meant a shopper could arrive on Canal Street on St. Charles Avenue or Royal Street, shop at the big stores in the 700, 800 and 900 blocks, then board the Canal line inbound (toward the river), transferring back to the route that took them into town. Day trippers could easily get from the train stations to the stores and back.

Henry Clay Monument, St. Charles Avenue, Royal and Canal Streets, 1893. *Library of Congress.*

There is something mystical about the intersection of Royal Street, Canal Street and St. Charles Avenue. In the late 1850s, the city decided this intersection would be the best place for a massive monument to Henry Clay. Patrons of Creole shops and businesses on Rue Royale emerged onto Canal Street to continue their shopping. Since 1835, streetcars carrying uptowners have dropped their passengers off where St. Charles met Canal. It was the ultimate convergence of New Orleans styles and cultures.

At the time of the opening of Maison Blanche Department Store in 1897, the stores stopped at Dauphine Street, but the streetcars kept going to Basin. There was room for one more big store in the Canal Street Zone.

3
Krauss Department Store

Leon Fellman was born Lippman Feibelman, in 1846, in Rülzheim, Germany. Lippman came to the United States, New Orleans, specifically, in 1864. His brother, Bernard Fellman, was already in New Orleans. Bernard had changed his last name to Fellman. Lippman did so as well, also changing his first name. Leon worked in several business concerns after settling in the city. On November 3, 1873, Bernard and Leon opened Fellman Brothers at 133 Canal Street, in the Touro Buildings, located in the middle of the block of buildings between Royal and Bourbon Streets.

The Fellman brothers were dry goods merchants. In an ad in the *Daily Picayune* on March 5, 1878, they declared, "We hereby tender a special invitation to strangers in our city, and the public in general, only to inspect the many novelties we are displaying, and that prices that will please the most economical buyer." They offered a wide variety of silk goods, as well as white goods, sheets and other fabrics. They also offered hosiery for women, men and children.

In 1881, the brothers moved the dry goods store a few doors down, to 129 Canal. The *Daily Picayune* reported that "they have arranged to retain the old store [133 Canal], which is to be devoted to the sale of ladies' suits, dolmans, cloaks, and the like, under management of Mr. Jules F. Dreyfus, a long time leading salesman of the house." The paper also explained the business philosophy of the concern, large sales and small profits.

Leon married Blanche Godchaux, daughter of local merchant Leon Godchaux, on Wednesday, February 10, 1886. Godchaux was a well-

Canal Street, looking up from St. Charles Avenue. The Touro Buildings are to the right, and the Mercier Building is in the background. *Library of Congress.*

established businessman and merchant. The ceremony was held at Temple Sinai, followed by a reception at the Godchaux family home, on Esplanade and Marais Streets, in Faubourg Marigny.

Fellman Brothers Dry Goods continued its success. The *Daily Picayune* marveled at the store's ability to slash prices and draw in customers, on August 14, 1887: "Never in the history of the firm has a steadier stream of humanity poured in than between Monday morning and Saturday evening. It fairly rained customers, and the great misfortune was a shortage of clerks." The paper noted that this incredible boost in business happened in the heat of the summer, while Leon was traveling, buying fall goods. David Haas, a junior partner in the firm, was left in charge of the staff. The weather in the city that August was exactly what one would expect. The writer for the *Picayune* expressed the desire of customers for "a fan, a revolving fan, to cool, and keep cool, the excitable souls who want a dress pattern from some extra cheap goods, before the last piece vanishes!"

Also in 1887, Fellman's advertised its cooperation with Red Star Shoes. The Red Star store was located just down the street from the Touro Buildings, at the corner of Canal and Exchange Place. By December, the brothers were slashing prices to the point where the *Picayune* again noted the uptick in activity at the store.

In 1888, Leon Fellman expressed a desire to relocate Fellman's from the Touro Buildings to the Mercier Building, on Dauphine and Canal. The Mercier Building was built in 1885, after Christ Episcopal Church auctioned off the property and moved to St. Charles Avenue and Sixth Streets, Uptown. Bernard Fellman wasn't interested in moving the business, so the brothers dissolved the partnership. They closed the Fellman's location at 133 Canal. The location at 129 Canal (later 727 Canal Street, when the city renumbered all the buildings on Canal, so they were by block, not building) became B. Fellman Dry Goods.

Some of the younger men Fellman's brought into the business were the Krausz brothers, Leopold, Max, Sigmund and Fritz. All four worked for Leon at one time or another. In 1887, Leopold and Sigmund, along with H.M.A. Langenfeld, opened Krausz and Langenfeld, in the 100 block of Bourbon Street. The store sold perfumes, kid gloves, some home furnishings and fancy goods. Langenfeld retired from the business in 1889.

L. Fellman and Company opened on September 30, 1889. David Haas continued in partnership with Leon, in the Mercier Building. They combined the stores in the building at 173, 175 and 177 Canal into one. The rest of the Mercier Building was leased by Simon J. Shwartz, after a fire severely damaged his father Abram's store, located on Canal, between Bourbon and Dauphine Streets.

The *Daily Picayune* reported that Fellman and Haas "fitted the entire premises with all modern conveniences, such as elevators, electric bells, gas chandeliers, counters, shelves, stools, offices, etc., and it now stands as one of the largest, best lighted, and best arranged business houses in the south." The store continued to offer stock like Fellman's. Fellman hired a staff of 150 clerks, floor-walkers (department managers), cash boys and others.

Leon and Blanche had one daughter, May, who was born on May 27, 1892. On September 3, 1892, Bernard Fellman passed away. His wife and children continued to operate B. Fellman's after his death.

The Krausz brothers (the spelling of the family name changed in 1903) moved their store from Bourbon to Canal in 1893. The *Daily Picayune* described the store in 1897 as "Fairyland brought within easy reach." The store continued to sell fancy goods. Unlike Fellman's, the Krausz brothers appealed to customers seeking higher-end products. "The salesroom is a veritable art parlor, as already stated, and there is probably not a woman, or a man, for that matter, either, who could spend many minutes in the

Newspaper ad for S.J. Shwartz & Co., 1895. The store was located next to Fellman's in the Mercier Building.

Krausz Bros. store, 833 Canal Street, 1897. *New Orleans Public Library.*

place without an uncontrollable desire to purchase something, no matter how small the price, so that something of the beauty may be retained and carried away." The store stocked decorative items, "The goods which ladies like to buy and put on the little shelves and tables in the parlor and hall, and the dainty china which makes the china closet an attraction are to be had there."

The glove department at Krausz Brothers was extensive. It was in the front of the store. Chairs were arranged in front of the glove cases so customers could relax while trying on the merchandise.

Max and Sigmund operated Krausz Brothers at 833 Canal Street until 1900. Citing poor health, they closed the store, leased the building to a jeweler and took an extended trip.

L. Fellman and Company encountered a serious complication in 1897. In January, S.J. Shwartz negotiated to lease the entire Mercier Building. He planned to open New Orleans's first department store on Canal and Dauphine. That meant L. Fellman & Company had to vacate the building in October. From March 1897 through that summer, the store offered deep discounts on merchandise, as Fellman and Haas planned their next move. They leased the Pickwick Hotel, at Carondelet and Canal Streets. It was reported that a "local cotton man" had purchased the hotel. After renovations, the store opened in October, about the same time Shwartz opened Maison Blanche Department Store. Fellman continued his aggressive, high-volume/low-profit business model. In 1901, David Haas passed away. L. Fellman & Company dissolved, and the store became simply Leon Fellman.

In early 1899, Leon made another real estate move, purchasing several buildings in the 1200 block of Canal Street, between Basin and Franklin Streets. By June 1899, Fellman engaged the firm of Denis, Danziger & Tessier as agents to lease those buildings. They were known at the time as "Fellman's Row" and described as "proximate to everything, they are suitable for any mercantile purpose." By 1901, Fellman had acquired all five of the buildings in the 1200 block. He applied for and received a building permit in December 1902, "for a two-story brick structure to be known

Royal Street, in the French Quarter, 1900. *Library of Congress.*

as the Fellman building, in the square bounded by Canal, Basin, Liberty and Customhouse streets, and to cost $21,000. John Minot, builder." The building was completed by the next spring. Fellman leased the building to Sam and Leopold Krausz (who changed their last name to "Krauss"). They were described as "enterprising young men…who went to school in the dry goods business and graduated under that able professor of the business, Mr.

Leon Fellman, so they are thoroughly instructed." The store was heralded as "the second revolutionary movement which has worked wonders for the Great Thoroughfare."

Building the store on the lake side of Canal and Basin was indeed revolutionary, for several reasons. First, it was on the other side of the railroad tracks that were the end of the line for the steam trains that went out to Spanish Fort on Lake Pontchartrain. That rail line was out of service in 1903, and the tracks would be taken over by the Southern Railroad in 1904. It's likely that Fellman knew of the plans to build a large passenger station in the middle of Canal and Basin Streets a year later.

The other reason Fellman's new building turned heads was because it was at the edge of the Storyville red-light district. The conventional wisdom of the time was that Canal Street shoppers weren't going to venture that close to Storyville. The *New Orleans Item* observed, "For some time there has been a tendency to expand the dry goods business on Canal Street, and the large stores have been moving slowly backwards on the street. No one, however, appeared to care to venture beyond Rampart Street until Mr. Leon Fellman, with the nerve requisite to carry out such a project, appeared on the scene." Fellman's move was poised to be profitable. He capitalized the venture, leased the building to ambitious merchants he knew capable of the task, then stepped back and let them run their store. On March 26, 1903, the store opened its doors. By the end of the month, Krauss announced its first ten-cent sale, held in the last week of its opening month.

Krauss Department Store, 1912. The original building built by Fellman was the two-story structure in the front. *Library of Congress.*

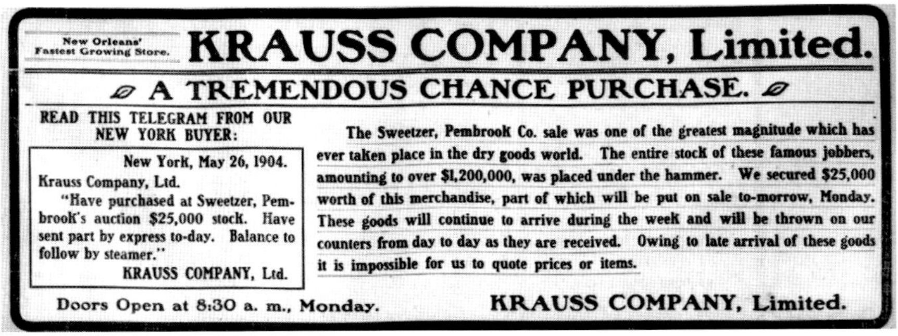

Krauss newspaper ad, in the *Daily Picayune*, 1904. *New Orleans Public Library*.

It didn't take long for Krauss to attract experienced staff. Sol Israel of Leon Fellman's joined Krauss in its second week to work in the clothing department, as did Curt Wunderlich, of Beekman. It was announced on April 26, 1903, that Albert Oppenheim of Maison Blanche joined Krauss to take charge of the lace and embroidery department. Also from MB, Miss Lilly Lobstein, came to 1201 Canal, as well as Miss G.I. Fornham, who worked at Kauffman & Isaacs. The new store also attracted experienced senior management. George Weiman became general superintendent of Krauss Company. He was the manager of the linen and white goods departments at Maison Blanche and worked in the housekeeping department of D.H. Holmes prior to that. These sorts of personnel changes were important to dry goods stores, since so much of a store's advertising and reputation was based on word-of-mouth. The "new and up-to-date trade center of New Orleans, the most modern store in the south," was poised to make a big splash on Canal Street.

Always looking for an innovation or an edge, Krauss began to sell grocery items in 1905, being the first department store to add a grocery department. The press reported the department was well received. The grocery department provided an amusing aside, on Saturday, September 2, 1905. The electric lights in the store failed for a few minutes, giving the cash boys a chance to sneak into the sugar barrels for a treat.

Business had grown at Krauss so much so that by 1906, management looked to expand the store. They hired Stone Brothers, architects, to draw up plans for a five-story expansion building that would attach to the rear of the existing building. It's interesting that in the spring of 1906, S.J. Shwartz was ready to demolish the Mercier Building. Maison Blanche was also taking construction bids in April 1906 to erect the building (also

Elk Place, 1905, shot from Canal and Basin Streets. *Library of Congress.*

designed by Stone) that would become their flagship store throughout the twentieth century and is now a Ritz-Carlton Hotel. Construction on the Krauss expansion was delayed and began in May 1911. Naturally, the store had a massive sale prior to construction to empty the warehouse behind the store of merchandise so it could be demolished.

It's not surprising that a store the size of Krauss would have problems with shoplifting and theft. In the early years of the store's operation, there were occasional reports of pickpockets, such as the one who stole $16 from Mrs. H. Vitter in 1906. Stockings appear to have been a popular item to steal. In 1908, an "old and shabbily dressed" woman was caught stealing stockings from Krauss. When she was searched, it turned out she had also stolen merchandise from D.H. Holmes. Also in 1908, an African American woman named Delphine Jousta, who lived at Peniston and Annunciation, Uptown, was caught after "she quietly slipped two pairs of stockings, worth 35 cents each, into her bosom." Delphine was caught by a clerk. A floor-walker took her to the business office on the second floor, but when she got out of the elevator, "she rushed to one of the open windows on the Basin

Street side of the building and jumped to the ground." She was taken to the hospital. These incidents were minor when compared to a burglary that took place at Krauss on Tuesday, January 16, 1912. Thieves broke into the store by climbing up a fire escape in the rear of the second floor. They evaded the night watchman and made off with $128.24 in coins from the cash drawers. Clearly, they were petty thieves, because they didn't attempt to break into the store safe, which contained $800.

Children's white lawn dresses were forty-nine cents each at Krauss in the spring of 1917. The store was now in its fourteenth year of operation, with the advertising motto, "We Never Knowingly Allow Anyone to Undersell Us." A year later, the store added automobile tires to its product line, becoming distributors for Blackstone Tires. It was observed that "this is the first movement among New Orleans department stores to enter the motor car field in any way, and may presage a general move among these establishments in that direction." (It did, as Maison Blanche and D.H. Holmes both entered the car care business after World War II.)

From the opening of the store, Krauss employees participated in baseball games, playing teams from other stores. These baseball games were regular weekend happenings and expanded into other activities, like bowling, in

Western Union telegram boy, crossing South Rampart Street at Canal Street, 1918. Krauss and Terminal Station are in the background. *Library of Congress.*

later years. The merchants played at various ballparks in the city. On June 15, 1918, the team from Marks Issac was defeated by Krauss, 7–1. There wasn't a regular league in the 1910s, with the store teams just challenging each other regularly.

Krauss survived the United States' brief involvement in World War I and the closing of the Storyville district. In 1920, business was booming, with "actual $20 suits" on sale for $10, and $20 and $25 dresses on sale for $10. The millinery department had "beautiful satin hats" for $2.98. The company reported day-after-Christmas sales were "the biggest business we have ever done, except this past Monday before Christmas, and it was almost equal to that."

The dynamics of management were changing at Krauss in 1920. Leon Fellman retired from active involvement in his own store, Leon Fellman's, in 1918. He observed that the Krauss brothers were losing interest in the day-to-day operations of the store. Fellman worked with Krauss brother-in-law Leon Heymann (husband of Thekla Krauss) to acquire a controlling interest in Krauss from the brothers and minority shareholders. Heymann was vice-president of the company, under Leopold Krauss.

Leon Fellman passed away on March 7, 1920. He left an estate of $1.7 million to his wife and daughter. On March 9, 1920, the *New Orleans Item* said of Fellman:

> *He bought right and sold right. He did business on the level and the profit which he took was a legitimate profit.*
>
> *We have moved in business into a period which differs very much from that which Leon Fellman confronted when he started. Modern business is complicated. Some of Fellman's pupils have far out-stripped the master in the size of their establishments and the volume of business done. But a training under Fellman was invaluable, as all will admit. He was a great and successful merchant. His word was as good as his bond. To those who knew him well, he was a genial, kindly man and a good friend, and withal a generous public-spirited citizen.*

On Thursday, July 1, 1920, Leopold Krauss was presented a "beautiful, genuine Morocco hand bag." The presentation was made by the oldest employee at Krauss, Mr. S. Meridier Sr. The employees, through Meridier, heaped praise on Leopold. Krauss then thanked the gathering. Leopold then turned over all operations to the new president of Krauss, Leon

Heymann, and embarked on an extensive European trip. Leopold kept up with the store's affairs throughout the next decade, but the torch had been passed to his brother-in-law. Heymann stepped up and was fully prepared to take the store forward into the future. In seventeen years, Krauss had transformed Canal Street. The Storyville district had been gone for three years. Expansion up Canal Street, past Faubourg Treme into Mid-City, was in full gear, as Sicilian families moved out beyond the French Quarter and Treme. Krauss was still the end of the mercantile section of Canal Street, but Canal had expanded fully down to City Park Avenue and the cemeteries, with the opening of St. Anthony of Padua Parish in 1915. The 1920s would be a new chapter for the store, bringing new challenges with a new family at the helm.

4

Treme, Storyville and Creoles

Down in the Treme,
Just me and my baby...
—*John Boutte, "Treme"*

When Leon Fellman made the decision to buy up the downtown side of the 1200 block of Canal Street, Faubourg Treme was a well-established neighborhood. Did he simply see Canal Street as a linear concept, or did he factor the neighborhood behind what would become Krauss Department Store into his calculations?

The 1200 block of Canal Street is part of the western boundary of Faubourg Treme, the neighborhood just north (toward the lake) from the Vieux Carré. For over a century after New Orleans was established, the area north of the city was undeveloped farmland. In 1788, the city constructed the first cemetery outside the Vieux Carré, now known as St. Louis Cemetery No. 1. The cemetery was built one block back from Rampart Street, the last street of the original city.

Just outside the ramparts that became Rampart Street, slaves would gather. Before the days when we could all run for air conditioning, escape into the department store or confine ourselves at home, people would gather together to socialize and try to beat the heat in the summer. In Spanish-controlled New Orleans of the late eighteenth century, this even applied to the slaves. Respecting Sunday as a day of rest, the Spanish gave their slaves the afternoon off and allowed them to socialize. Like the rest of us, slaves in New Orleans gathered and complained about the heat. They also entertained themselves, making music and dancing.

The city leaders allowed the slaves to congregate outside the city, in an open area just outside the original city, north of Rampart Street. This area became known as the Place des Nègres, more commonly as Place Congo. By the time the Americans took control, the city had grown past the Vieux Carré, and this gathering point was called Congo Square. Congo Square was the place where black slaves could once again be Africans, even if for just one afternoon a week. They would bring drums, bells and other musical instruments to the square and gather, roughly by tribe, to play music, sing and dance.

What separated New Orleans from the British colonies was the more laid-back attitude of the French and Spanish in terms of treatment of slaves. The Catholics in New Orleans followed the old Code Noir (Black Code), which was a much less harsh overall set of guidelines than what the Protestant British followed. Additionally, the Catholics, even the Spanish, usually did not concern themselves with the "African" aspects of slave life and culture that their slaves kept. The British planters demanded their slaves take up Christianity (and the slaves did so, at least in outward forms), and African-based music, song and dance were not permitted. These trends continued after the American Revolution by the original states. When New Orleans became part of the United States, it took time for American ways to merge with the Continental philosophy.

Around 1795, Claude Tremé purchased the plantation to the east of the newly constructed Carondelet Canal. Tremé followed the lead of Bernard Marigny (who owned the plantation just downriver from the city) and subdivided his land, selling lots to potential homeowners. By the 1840s, French-Spanish Creoles and the gens de couleur libres (free people of color) turned the Tremé plantation into a faubourg, a neighborhood. St. Augustine Parish was founded in 1841. Since Congo Square had established the neighborhood as a main focal point for African culture, it was no surprise the church parish in the neighborhood blended into that focal point.

The Sunday afternoon gatherings in Congo Square continued well into the 1880s, despite being banned in the 1840s. By this time, Fellman was well established on Canal Street, and the Krauss brothers were learning the trade from him. After the Civil War, white city leaders tried to suppress the gatherings, even going as far as officially renaming Place Congo Beauregard Square, after former CSA general (and postwar civic leader)

Krauss and Terminal Station on Canal Street, 1912. Storyville is behind Krauss. *Library of Congress.*

P.G.T. Beauregard. The residents of the Vieux Carré and Faubourg Treme, however, always referred to the area as Congo Square.

Faubourg Treme was defined primarily by transportation, being a nexus of street railways, railroads and the Carondelet Canal. It was long considered a "backatown" neighborhood. The combination of train tracks, turning basin and cemeteries isolated most of Treme from Canal Street. Since the established Creole neighborhood was on the east side of the canal, the area to its west, up to Canal Street, did not bond with the east side. That isolation meant there was little neighborhood pushback when entrepreneurs wanted to open restaurants, saloons and even brothels. The area was truly the wrong side of the tracks.

Perhaps this factored into Fellman's move to acquire the 1200 block of Canal. Yes, the notion of expanding the city's High Street was appealing, but it also had to be sustainable. Fellman was bold, but not reckless. His original two-story store building would not be large enough to compete with Maison Blanche or even his own store at Canal and Carondelet. Just three years after Krauss opened, S.J. Shwartz began the process of tearing down his building and constructing a newer, larger store. The Krauss brothers were able to do the same thing, since Fellman had acquired the land behind the store, going down Basin Street, past Bienville. Without neighborhood activists to stop him, it was easy to demolish the houses behind the store, allowing Krauss to expand over time. The first Krauss expansion of 1906 set the stage for the store to become one of the largest in town.

In addition to physically expanding the store itself, it was important that people be able to get to Krauss. The transit hub at Canal and Rampart was only a block away. The train tracks on Basin Street didn't help bring people to the store at first, but when the passenger railroad terminal was built in the Basin Street neutral ground in 1908, Krauss was in a perfect position to cater to folks just arriving in town. A savvy businessman such as Fellman surely would have known about these plans as they developed. Later, the second generation of Krauss management, led by Leon Heymann, observed the growth of automobile ownership. They still relied on public transit to bring people to the store, but the trend of taking a car downtown was beginning. It was important for any retail concern to provide parking for customers. The western section of Faubourg Treme made it easy for Krauss to acquire land for parking lots and garages.

At the time Fellman was eyeing property in the area, Treme was quite different from the Vieux Carré and Central Business District. It was considered to be an unrefined neighborhood. In the early 1890s, merchants

Krauss (*left*) and Terminal Station, 1910. *Library of Congress.*

and other leaders in the Vieux Carré wanted to rid their neighborhood of gambling parlors, saloons and prostitution. Their solution was simple: designate an area in the city where these pursuits would be legal and come down hard on those who engaged in those pursuits outside of the legal district. Sidney Story, a member of the city council, proposed to create a red-light district. The district was bounded by Customhouse (later Iberville), Basin, St. Louis and North Robertson Streets. Much to Sidney's chagrin, folks began to refer to his proposed red-light district as "Storyville," or the "Storyville District."

Story's Ordinance No. 13,032 became law in 1897 and was affirmed by the courts after three years of legal challenges. It stated:

> *That from the first of October, 1897, it shall be unlawful for any public prostitute or woman notoriously abandoned to lewdness to occupy, inhabit, live or sleep in any house, room, or closet, situated without the following limits: South side of Custom House street from Basin to Robertson street, east side of Robertson street from Custom House to St. Louis street, from Robertson to Basin street. Provided, That no lewd woman shall be permitted to occupy a house, room, or closet on St. Louis street. Provided further, That nothing herein shall be so construed as to authorize any lewd woman to occupy a house, room, or closet in any portion of the city.*

Brothels, ranging from inexpensive rooms (cribs) to elegant homes, began to appear. It wasn't enough to have brothels in the district, however. Men who patronized the sporting clubs needed a more palatable reason for being in the district. Barkeeps like Tom Anderson, who ran a popular saloon on North Rampart Street, opened establishments in Storyville. Anderson's Arlington Cafe, named after the well-known madam Josie Arlington, was located on the corner of Customhouse and Basin, right behind Krauss Department Store.

The wonderful form of music we know as jazz did not originate in Storyville, as many believe, but the district nurtured the music and its players. The upscale sporting clubs would hire piano players to offer light music in their parlors before the couples went upstairs. Some of these houses would even hire fledgling jazz combos to entertain the clients. The saloons in Storyville were also looking to attract customers, and the owners of those joints knew live music was a winner even then. Buddy Bolden, Jelly Roll Morton, Pops Foster and a host of other early jazz musicians performed in the brothels and saloons of Storyville. A young Louis Armstrong earned money by hauling

Unidentified Storyville prostitute, photographed by E.J. Bellocq, around 1900. *New Orleans Public Library*.

coal to the brothels and saloons. This gave him the opportunity to listen to the musicians playing in the saloons. Armstrong later said Joe "King" Oliver was his first horn teacher, a relationship likely formed while Oliver was performing in Storyville.

There has been a great deal written about Storyville, much of which is quite distorted from reality. Prostitution, the "oldest profession," was far from romantic on a day-to-day basis. While the sporting clubs along Basin Street were opulently appointed and employed the most attractive and desirable of the ladies of Storyville, the houses off Basin, on Liberty, Marais and Villere Streets, rented out cribs to women who charged significantly less than Josie Arlington's girls. These women worked long hours and made little money but still had to keep up appearances to attract customers. A store offering deep discounts was a welcome addition to the neighborhood. They could buy stockings, fabric, buttons and fasteners for dresses, as well as "fancy lingerie," at discounted prices at Krauss. The women working at the better houses could purchase dresses rather than make them, as well as patronize the store's millinery department, buying the latest hats. Their presence in the neighborhood made them a credit to their various places of employment, as well as living advertisements for Krauss.

It's important to mention that Storyville was not the only red-light district in New Orleans at this time. The original goal of Story's ordinances was to get prostitution out of the Vieux Carré, and in that respect, the district was successful. Then mayor Martin Behrman was fond of saying of the business, "You can make it illegal, but you can't make it unpopular."

The establishments of Storyville catered exclusively to a white clientele. African American men who were interested in engaging ladies for some pleasure were barred from the houses of the district. They were required to patronize houses and cribs on the Uptown side of Canal, mostly located around South Rampart and Basin Streets. This area became known as Black Storyville. The ladies working in Black Storyville had the same issues in terms of attracting clients and had even less money to work with.

One of the most popular sporting palaces of the district was Mahogany Hall, located on Basin Street. Mahogany Hall was operated by Lulu White. White, originally from Selma, Alabama, was an African American woman and one of the most well-known personalities in Storyville. In 1912, White opened a saloon at 1200 Bienville Street. This was in the block between Bienville and Canal Street. The saloon remained in business past Prohibition, switching to being a soft drink bar. The saloon was raided periodically by law enforcement. Lulu White retired from the saloon business in 1929 when she sold her establishment to Leon Heymann. Heymann converted it into a maintenance building for Krauss.

The experiment of Storyville ended abruptly in 1917. The entry of the United States into World War I meant New Orleans would be a major point of departure for soldiers and sailors going to Europe. The secretaries of the army and navy at the time made a grand show of the moral might of

The "Arlington Annex," owned by the "Mayor of Storyville," Tom Anderson, Custom House and Bienville Streets, 1900. *New Orleans Public Library.*

"Down the Line" on Basin Street. Anderson's Arlington Annex is on the corner, with the "Sporting Palaces" extending down for several blocks. *New Orleans Public Library.*

This grocery store is one of the last remaining Storyville buildings. *Carlos "Froggy" May.*

U.S. forces. To that end, the military prohibited the operation of brothels within five miles of army posts. Downtown New Orleans was not a military establishment, but many of the men heading to Europe came to the ships docked at the Port of New Orleans via trains that terminated their journeys at Canal and Basin Streets. All those soldiers had to do was walk across the street, and they were presented with the saloons and brothels of the district.

This became not only a moral but also a public health concern for the military. Mayor Behrman bowed to intense pressure from Washington and ordered the district closed in November 1917. Prostitution was once again illegal in all neighborhoods of New Orleans. A number of the houses of the district remained in operation into the 1920s, but discreetly.

All this happened right behind Fellman's Row, later Krauss. The activities of the district surely did not go unnoticed by the business one block in front of it. Still, the well-deserved reputation of Storyville did not deter customers from shopping at Krauss. With the streetcars dropping them off at Rampart and Canal, all they had to do was walk past the train station and they were there.

Storyville is far from the entire tale of Faubourg Treme. The character of the neighborhood changed completely once one walked down past the turning basin and Congo Square. New Orleans's oldest African American neighborhood was a strong community. Many of the residents of Treme spoke French as their primary language. Since the 1830s, the Treme Market, located on Orleans Avenue at Marais Street, had been one of the city's most active public markets. Even though the traffic through the Carondelet Canal steadily declined in the late 1800s and early 1900s, the turning basin was still active with fishermen and oystermen who brought their catches to market. There were numerous light-industrial businesses along the canal, providing jobs to men in the neighborhood.

As time went on in Treme, racial lines began to blur. Whites married free people of color; those folks married into other white and mixed families. By Reconstruction, it was often quite difficult to tell who was black and who was white.

Many families who descended from the original free people of color considered themselves separate from freed slaves. About this time, the meaning of the term *Creole* began to expand. Creoles were those who descended from the French and Spanish residents of the city and was used to contrast them from the Anglo Irish Americans and German immigrants. As Treme became more and more mixed, so did Creole.

Today, it's tough to pin down a definition of Creole. Restaurateur Wayne Baquet Sr. has a significant Krauss connection—he ran the luncheonette at

Aerial view of Storyville, 1905. *Library of Congress.*

the store as Eddie's at Krauss (an homage to his father, Eddie Baquet) in the 1980s. Let's consider his definition:

> *The real Creole people of New Orleans is a mixture of the French, Spanish, American Indian and African, because these are the people that inhabited New Orleans back in the day. And they had to intermingle to survive, and that's what happened. That's why when you come to New Orleans, you see black folks with all these different colors. Some of them you can't even tell what they are. Some of them look Oriental, some of them look white, some of them look black, you know, all mixtures of colors because of this total mixture, this melding pot mixture, this gumbo of people that we have including—and then as time went on, we even had the Italian input, you know. So all of that mixed together—these are the people in New Orleans, and that's what I am—me and my family result—that's what the Creole people are.*

Yes, "all that mixed together" is a great way to define Creole. It's a great way to describe Treme when the Krauss brothers opened their store. The building may have been owned by one Jewish merchant and the store operated by a second Jewish family, but the neighborhood was all mixed. New Orleanians from all over the city could take streetcars to get to Krauss, but the Creoles could walk.

And walk they did, attracted by the low prices offered at Krauss. Creoles purchased "piece goods," such as fabrics, to create their own up-to-date fashions. There was work in Treme, and work meant disposable income. Krauss was more than happy to have the Creoles spend their money on Canal Street.

There were complications to operating a store serving a mixed-race neighborhood in the 1900s. Ironically, the actions of members of the Treme community had national ramifications. In 1890, the State of Louisiana passed the Louisiana Railway Accommodations Act, commonly referred to as the Separate Car Act. The act was designed to segregate passenger rail coaches by race.

> *An Act to promote the comfort of passengers on railway trains; requiring all railway companies carrying passengers on their trains, in this State, to provide equal but separate accommodations for the white and colored races, by providing separate coaches or compartments so as to secure separate accommodations; defining the duties of the officers of such railways;*

> *directing them to assign passengers to the coaches or compartment set aside for the use of the race to which such passengers belong; authorizing them to refuse to carry on their train such passengers as may refuse to occupy the coaches or compartments to which he or she is assigned; to exonerate such railway companies from any and all blame or damages that might proceed or result from such a refusal; to prescribe penalties for all violations of this act; to put this act into effect ninety days after its promulgation, and to repeal all laws or parts of laws contrary to or inconsistent with the provisions of this act.*

This was one of the first "separate but equal" laws enacted in the United States. Treme being the nexus of the black community, it was only natural that opposition to the law would germinate there. Community leaders formed the *Comité des Citoyens* (Citizens Committee—remember, much of Treme was French-speaking). A young man named Homer Plessy was recruited to test the law. Plessy was an octoroon, meaning he was one-eighth black. Plessy's grandfather was a Frenchman named Germain Plessy. Germain married Catherine Mathieu, a free woman of color. His father, Joseph Adolphe Plessy, married a white woman, Rosa Debergue. Homer's light skin allowed him to "pass," like many residents of Treme. Homer, a shoemaker like his father, would have easily blended in with the white shoppers on Canal Street.

L. Fellman & Company opened as usual on Tuesday, June 7, 1892, in the Mercier Building on Canal Street. On the other side of Faubourg Marigny, Homer Plessy bought a ticket on a train bound for Covington, Louisiana, the seat of St. Tammany Parish, on the north shore of Lake Pontchartrain. After purchasing a ticket in the whites-only first-class car, he declared that he was indeed black (legally, his grandmother's race passed down to him). He was arrested, and by 1896, the U.S. Supreme Court, in the case *Plessy v. Ferguson*, declared "separate but equal" to be the law of the land.

It was certainly legal for merchants like the Krauss brothers to sell their wares to people of all races, but they were required to segregate various facilities, such as restrooms and drinking fountains. In spite of these Jim Crow laws, Krauss Department Store regularly hired African Americans. Those employees ate lunch in a separate employee dining room and used separate restrooms, but they were still an important part of the Krauss community and culture. The porters who cleaned the store were black, as were many of the seamstresses who created the custom clothing, bedding items, curtains and draperies sold by the store.

African American shoppers on Canal Street learned to adapt to Jim Crow restrictions. By the time Krauss opened, the store's black customers rode to the store in the back of streetcars and used segregated restrooms where they could. It wasn't easy at times, but life went on. Certainly, many of the Creoles of Treme continued to defy the laws and ordinances created to segregate New Orleans, passing as white. Krauss Department Store was locked in competition with the other downtown merchants. It was natural for residents of Treme to take the path of least resistance, walking a few blocks from the eastern side of Congo Square to the store closest to them.

As African Americans began to chafe under the restrictions of Jim Crow laws in the southern states, many families gave up on those states, migrating north. This migration had a significant impact on Faubourg Treme. As black families prepared to give up on New Orleans, they needed to sell their homes in Treme. White folks who favored segregation were not terribly interested in moving into a mixed neighborhood, but black homeowners readily found buyers in the city's Sicilian community. Since the 1880s, Sicilians had arrived in New Orleans in large numbers. By the 1910s, they dominated the Vieux Carré and Faubourg Treme. The Sicilians were legally white, but many of the Anglo Irish residents considered them of a lower caste. Still, segregation didn't apply to them, and they considered New Orleans a good place to live. The French Market and Treme Market took on a decided Italian flavor in the 1900s. The departure of African Americans opened up opportunities for not only the Sicilians but also Serbs and Croat families.

The years following World War I were overall prosperous ones for New Orleans. Still, most of the Sicilians were first- and second-generation immigrants in those early years of Krauss. They worked as laborers or were struggling to start businesses in the community. With little disposable income, it was important to these families to be frugal. The price-slashing ways of the Canal Street merchants appealed to everyone on a tight budget. The Sicilians joined the Creoles in taking advantage of the Krauss brothers' price competition with Fellman, as well as Shwartz at Maison Blanche and the Godchauxs. The city had evolved a great deal in just the first two decades Krauss was open.

5

Heymann at the Helm

I said a New Orleans woman,
She's alright with me.
That's my hometown I'm talking about.
—Louis Armstrong and his All-Stars, "Tin Roof Blues"

Leon Heymann was an experienced dry goods merchant when he took over Krauss Department Store. Born in New Orleans on May 16, 1883, his father, Henry Heymann, was from Plotsk, Poland. Henry married a French immigrant, Caroline Rosenthal. They had two sons, Leon and Maurice. Henry was a merchant, described as a "peddler." His sons followed him into business, apprenticing with local Jewish merchants.

Like many young Jewish men, Leon Heymann began a career in retailing. He met Thekla Krauss, sister of the successful Krauss brothers. On June 12, 1906, three years after the Krauss brothers opened their store on Canal Street, Leon and Thekla were married. They moved to Houma, Louisiana.

In 1907, Maurice and Leon decided to leverage their basic knowledge of French by opening a store in Houma, Louisiana. The Cajun communities of southeast Louisiana mainly spoke French, which isolated towns like Houma and Thibodaux from New Orleans at the turn of the twentieth century. The Heymanns opened the Houma Bargain Store in the Heymann Building on Main Street. Heymann's store suffered a serious setback on December 1, 1911, when a fire caused $10,000 worth of damage to the building and burned $25,000 of retail stock. Heymann was undeterred;

The Thibodaux 5 & 10 Cent Store, 1908. *Krauss Collection, University of New Orleans Earl K. Long Library.*

he opened in a temporary building while the store was rebuilt. Around 1909, Maurice moved to Lafayette, Louisiana, and built a significant retail empire in that city.

Leon Heymann became active in the community in Houma. He was a member of the Elks Lodge and a founding member of the Terrebone Rod and Gun Club, in 1919. He expanded his business interests to Thibodaux, Louisiana, opening a store there. Heyman's stores operated several delivery and service trucks, and Firestone Tires was proud to include his name in ads featuring customer endorsements.

Even though he and Thekla lived a just a couple hours from the city, Leon Heymann was still a Krauss brother-in-law. In 1918, he negotiated with Leon Fellman to buy his stake in the store and acquire shares from minority holders who were not family members. The Fellman family retained ownership of the 1201 Canal Street building. By 1921, Krauss was wholly owned by the family. Thekla and Leon returned to New Orleans, and Leon took his place in the management of the store, working for Leopold Krauss. When Leopold decided to take an extended vacation to Europe in 1920, he gave the keys to Leon Heymann. Leon assumed the title of president the following year.

Once his position with Krauss was secured, Heymann then moved to divest his holdings down the bayou. He sold the stores in Thibodaux and Houma. Management of the Houma Bargain Store passed from Leon to J.W. Bojarski, a Russian immigrant. Bojarski managed the store into the 1950s. The Heymann family retained ownership of the Main Street building, eventually donating the property to the City of Houma when the store closed in the 1970s.

In March 1921, employees of Krauss formed the Krauss Employees' Benevolent Association. They held a day trip and picnic fundraiser in June of that year. On June 24, 1922, the *New Orleans States* reported that the association would hold a second picnic outing, taking the early morning Orleans-Kenner Railroad interurban to the farming community of Kenner, Louisiana (now the location of Louis Armstrong New Orleans International Airport), where there would be food, fun, games and entertainment from the Tuxedo band. The association expected three hundred guests to attend. Clearly, the outing was a success, since the association advertised another outing the following June, featuring music from Kid Rena's Jazz band. The association had an arrangement with an excursion riverboat, the SS *Capitol*, which regularly scheduled dance cruises for the group. The house band on the steamer at the time was organized by jazz legend Fate Marable; it's likely that the Krauss employees were treated to the cornet stylings of a young Louis Armstrong, cruising on the river.

Krauss Department Store, 1921. *Krauss Collection, University of New Orleans Earl K. Long Library.*

Riverboat SS *Capitol*, 1923. *Library of Congress.*

Women's bloomers sold for $0.15 a pair at Krauss in November 1921. The store aggressively promoted home furnishings that fall, advertising sales on velvet rugs, as well as Axminster and Brussels rugs and, for the first time, Wilton rugs. Lace curtains were $1.50 a pair, and the store's staff of seamstresses were more than able to do custom curtain jobs for the housewives of New Orleans.

The twentieth year of operation for Krauss was one of major changes and upgrades. First, Heymann negotiated an extension on the lease on the store building, which was owned by Mrs. May Fellman Parker (Leon Fellman's daughter). Then he made personal real estate acquisitions to secure the rest of the block bounded by Canal, Franklin, Customhouse and Basin Streets. Heymann leased the land to the store and began a $500,000 expansion and upgrade project. An additional five-story expansion was constructed behind the 1911 building. The windows and showcases facing Canal Street were enlarged. New flooring was installed throughout the store. Krauss also purchased and installed New Orleans's first escalator, connecting the ground floor with the mezzanine. It was just an "up" escalator; shoppers had to take the stairs back down.

Department store advertising was usually straightforward in the 1920s. Newspaper ads were the mainstay of the strategy. The stores paid enough for daily ads that the papers would run various small feature stories about events and activities in the store as well. Sometimes, a perfect feature story falls right into an advertising manager's lap. Such was the case in April 1922, when Edward Schwartz, advertising manager for Krauss, received an interesting letter.

"Enclosed please find $7.50 for a coat that I bought in 1918. At the time of the purchase, I took the ticket off of a $15 coat and put it on a $22.50 coat. The $7.50 is the difference in the price. The coat wore so well that I feel I ought to pay you." Schwartz didn't miss the opportunity, as he got the *New Orleans States* to publish the story.

Canal Street was occasionally a place for excitement. On Saturday, September 27, 1924, two men hired a car on North Rampart and Iberville (just a block from Krauss) and asked to be taken to Baronne and Julia Streets, in the CBD. They were headed to a "soft drink establishment," many of which were speakeasies. Instead of taking them to the bar, the driver stopped in front of Krauss and demanded money. When the passengers refused, the driver threw one of them into the front window of the store and drove off. Replacing the window cost Krauss $150.

When the store's ownership was restructured into Krauss Company Ltd., Sam Krauss left the business. He opened a new store in 1923, at 227 Canal. Unfortunately, the store was robbed on September 10, 1924. When they caught up with the burglar, they found over two hundred men's shirts in his house. When $975 went missing from a desk at Krauss in June, some of the employees noticed that one of the porters, Charles Cook, had been on a major buying spree, purchasing a new suit, an expensive watch, a ring and other items. Cook also got married. The activity eventually led to his arrest for the theft.

Another addition in 1924 was the Optical Department, which sold eyeglasses. In 1926, the department was staffed by Dr. Chas. Staley, optometrist, and Lawrence Voss, optician. Examinations were free. Frames ranged in price from $.95 to $8.

Neither Heymann nor his predecessors at Krauss were experienced with shoe sales. The Fellmans would regularly do cross-promotions with nearby shoe stores at their store in the Touro Buildings, and Krauss didn't sell shoes for the first twenty years. That changed in 1924 with the opening of a huge shoe department on the ground floor. The front display windows were loaded with some of the over twenty thousand pairs of shoes brought in to kick off the full-service shoe department. This made "the largest display of shoes New Orleans has ever seen,"

Jake and Angie Ross at the Krauss employees' picnic, 1928. *Krauss Collection, University of New Orleans Earl K. Long Library.*

according to the *New Orleans States*. Seventy-five seats were set up in the department, which was staffed by forty clerks. Heymann brought in a contractor from San Antonio to manage the department. Katz told the press, "The aim of this part of the Krauss business will be to conform in all respects to the policies of every other department—the best of service, complete satisfaction, and popular prices on merchandise of fine quality. We know what good shoes are and how to buy them to give the public the benefit of lower prices." The store aggressively advertised the new department throughout October and November.

The store's Benevolent Association continued to be active in the mid-1920s, holding regular dances on the steamer *Capitol*. In 1924, one trip was a long day cruise down the river to Fort St. Philip, 176 miles, round-trip. The baseball team was also quite busy in the spring and summer, playing teams from other stores in the city. When the Krauss team handily beat a semi-pro team sponsored by Elmer's Candy, the Elmer's Sweetums, Elmer's decided to disband the team. They reorganized as an all-employee team, the Kandy Kids.

Candy was a theme in the store's marketing in 1925. For Easter, Krauss presented a young woman dressed as Little Miss Muffet in the Canal Street display window, giving away candy and balloons. The promotion was considered such a success that the store reprised it in October. Little Miss Muffet returned to the front window, this time with a six-foot-tall, two-hundred-pound peppermint stick, provided by the Altmont Candy Company. Altmont also provided individual candies that were given to kids who came by to see the display. This was a great way to get parents who might have started their shopping day down at D.H. Holmes or Maison Blanche to walk farther up the street to Krauss. Miss Muffet also made regular appearances in the store's millinery department, where Little Miss Muffet brand hats were sold. This promotion continued annually through 1929.

Krauss continued to expand in 1927, extending the building again. In addition to creating more floor space for all departments over the five floors, employee facilities on the fifth floor and the roof were upgraded. Two employee cafeterias (one for whites, the other for African Americans) and an executive dining room were opened, all serviced from the same kitchen and walk-in refrigerator. Rest room and lounge facilities for employees were also expanded and upgraded. A rooftop promenade was constructed "to give a better view—the beautiful panorama of the city of New Orleans can be seen stretching from the misty curve of the Mississippi River to the still more hazy boundary line of Lake Pontchartrain," according to the *New Orleans States*. Another significant addition to employee services was the construction of an infirmary on the fifth floor.

More innovation inside Krauss took place in 1927, when it was announced that the store would expand the Optical Department, for the sale of "Kodaks and supplies, developing films, and watch repairing." Krauss made it clear that the existing department staff would be retained and that the expansion into photographic supplies would not impair sales of eyeglasses. The department was created in 1924. An optometrist and an optician, along with sales clerks, staffed the counters. Free eye examinations were provided, and a wide variety of frames were sold. In 1927, shell frames with lenses sold for $1.45, while "genuine Kryptoks" sold for $7.95 a pair, with lenses. The optical department was located right next to the new music department.

Several other retail departments were added that year as well. A barbershop/beauty parlor, with six stylists for women and two barbers for men, opened on the second-floor mezzanine. A flower shop was opened in

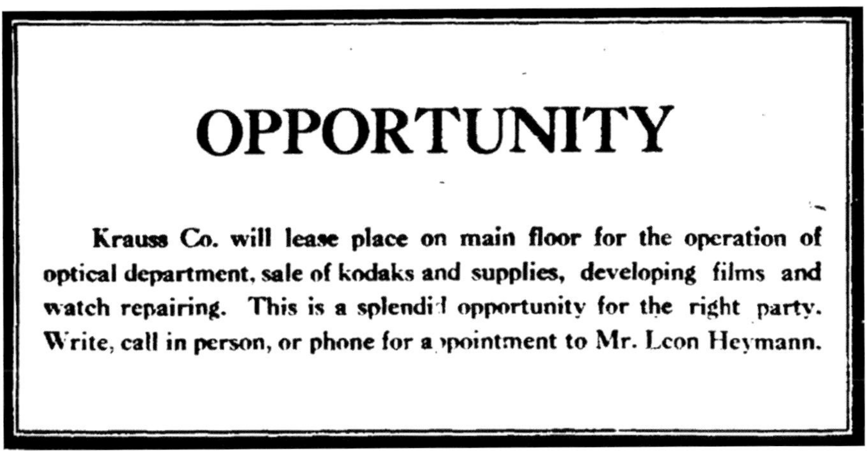

OPPORTUNITY

Krauss Co. will lease place on main floor for the operation of optical department, sale of kodaks and supplies, developing films and watch repairing. This is a splendid opportunity for the right party. Write, call in person, or phone for appointment to Mr. Leon Heymann.

Krauss newspaper ad, 1924. Leon Heymann began plans to expand the Optical Department that year. *New Orleans Public Library*.

the rear of the first floor, by the elevators, staffed by "experienced florists." The flower shop sold cut flowers as well as seeds and bulbs. Sales of furniture were greatly expanded, as the furniture department now took over almost the entire fourth floor.

Krauss went for twenty-three years without electric signage on the front of the store. While the store was festooned with electric lights for Carnival season annually in the 1910s, the store itself had not installed the large signs seen at other stores. That changed after Christmas in 1926. The store installed a forty-two-foot-high, five-foot-wide vertical sign spelling KRAUSS. The sign contained over 350 light bulbs. Locals observed that the combination of the Loews Theater's sign on one side and the Krauss sign on the other side of Canal and Basin really lit up the block.

In the late 1920s, Krauss departments were laid out as follows:

First Floor: Men's/Boy's, Piece Goods, Hosiery, Optical, Cut Flowers, Shoes, Candy, and other departments
First Mezzanine: Shoe Repair, Delivery Department, Reception Room
Second Mezzanine: Barbershop, Beauty Parlor.
Second Floor: Women's Departments
Third Floor: Home Furnishings
Fourth Floor: Furniture, General Offices, Credit Department
Fifth Floor: Wholesale Orders, Reserve Stock, Employee Cafeterias, Rest Rooms, Refrigeration Plant, Laundry.

In addition to these physical additions and upgrades, Krauss also implemented financial services for their customers. In September 1927, the store introduced the Krauss Club Plan for purchases of home furnishings and furniture. The plan's terms were a 20 percent down payment, with the customer making payments on the balance for eight months. This credit was extended with a 5 percent service charge. The marketing strategy behind the club plan was to put the finance charges out in the open, rather than burying the charges into overall higher prices, as they claimed other stores did.

Family news kicked off 1929, as May Heymann married Leon Wolf in January. Wolf also became part of the Krauss management team, working for May's father, Leon. Leon Heymann made an incredible real estate acquisition in September 1929, just before the stock market crash. He purchased the Audubon Building, located at the corner of Canal and Burgundy Streets. The purchase was based on a solid business strategy. While Heymann had acquired all the land behind the original Fellman building at

Leon M. Wolf Jr., 1925. *Krauss Collection, University of New Orleans Earl K. Long Library.*

1201 Canal, that building was still owned by May Fellman Parker. Heymann negotiated a twenty-year extension on the lease of the store's front in 1923. When the Audubon Building presented itself, it was an attractive way to secure the future of Krauss. To avoid being boxed into an unfavorable position when the 1201 Canal lease came up in 1943, Heymann now had a location to which Krauss could be moved.

In 1906–7, Isidore Newman and his son, Hart, had acquired the lot at Burgundy and Canal, with the intention of building a hotel on the property. The hotel idea fell through, and the Newmans sold the property. An office building was constructed in 1910, just after the completion of the Maison Blanche Building. F.W. Woolworth leased the ground floor of the building and opened a store there in 1916. As a business venture, however, the Audubon Building was not successful, forcing the owner, William Mason Smith, to sell.

Knowing the Woolworth lease would expire in 1940, Heymann had an ace in the hole for his own lease negotiations. Heymann made another aggressive Canal Street real estate purchase the following year, acquiring the Trianon Theater Building at 814 Canal. Leon continued to lease the building, located in between the Leon Fellman Building at 812 Canal and the Boston Club on its lake side, to various concerns.

The stock market crash of 1929 and the beginning of the Great Depression hit New Orleans and the state of Louisiana hard. With numerous businesses folding in the wake of the crash, activity at the port dropped dramatically. This created massive unemployment. Former governor Huey P. Long, now a U.S. senator, worked hard to steer many federal infrastructure and construction projects to Louisiana after taking his seat in that body in January 1929. Long's efforts helped blunt the impact of the first two years of the Great Depression. By the time the various programs of the New Deal began to take effect in the mid-1930s, New Orleans was on much more solid footing than much of the nation. The core philosophy of Krauss—quality merchandise at very low prices—carried the store through the Depression. As the decade went on, Krauss's pricing and service attracted many locals who were doing their best to stretch a dollar. For example, more and more

Krauss becomes the first store in New Orleans with store-wide air conditioning, May 11, 1931. *New Orleans Public Library.*

engagement announcements in the newspapers included photos of the brides-to-be that were taken at the Krauss photo studio.

Two big improvements to Krauss took place in 1931. On May 11, Krauss became the first department store in the city to air condition all of its retail space. This was "made possible by the beneficent activity of a 200-ton refrigerating plant, plus 28 motor-driven air supply fans and 4 pumps." This system kept the store at an even seventy-five degrees, while the temperature outside on Canal Street would regularly go above ninety degrees. Daily newspaper ads featured the block-letter Krauss logo covered in icicles that summer.

Krauss entered the radio and electrical appliances market on August 1, 1931. The store hired Bob Ham, a popular radio expert from Maison Blanche, as the department's first manager and buyer. Ham was a regular announcer for programs sponsored by Maison Blanche on WSMB radio. The call letters "WSMB" stood for "Sanger-Maison Blanche," the owners of the radio station, which was located on the top floor of the MB building at Dauphine and Canal. The store regularly promoted radio sales throughout the 1930s, including offering tube-testing service to owners needing their radios repaired. The radio department augmented the music department (selling pianos and phonographs) that had been in operation since 1927.

Store-wide air conditioning made another new feature for Krauss possible: a lunch counter. Operating a kitchen inside the retail space would have generated entirely too much heat, but the air-conditioning system made it possible to keep a kitchen cool. This original soda fountain/luncheonette was located on the first mezzanine. It had thirty-three feet of counter space, with "Pullman seats, upholstered in genuine red leather." The Krauss Luncheonette was a fixture on Canal Street from its opening until the store closed in 1997. When it opened, the luncheonette was billed primarily as a soda fountain that sold sandwiches.

Krauss was closed for two days in 1935, in tribute to two family members who passed away. Leon Heymann's mother, Caroline Rosenthal Heymann, passed away on February 13, 1935. The store closed again, on Friday, April 26, to mark the passing of its first president, Leopold Krauss, the day before. Leopold was survived by all of his brothers. The next to pass away was Samuel, in 1937.

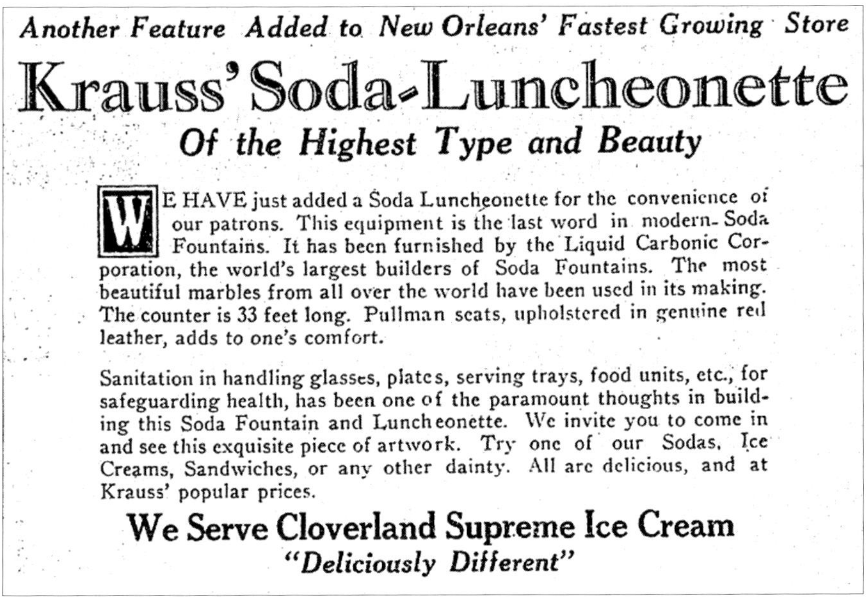

The Krauss Luncheonette opened on May 11, 1931. *New Orleans Public Library.*

Shoppers at Krauss, 1932. *Krauss Collection, University of New Orleans Earl K. Long Library.*

The banking industry of the United States went through dramatic restructuring during the Great Depression. Whitney National Bank of New Orleans worked through this process to continue to this day. Leon Heymann was one of the directors of the bank in the mid-1930s, supervising the bank's officers as they joined the Federal Deposit Insurance Corporation.

Krauss was one of those companies where folks worked for their entire career. That made it even sadder when a member of the staff passed away. George Griener had worked in the delivery department at Krauss since 1905, and he died at his home in uptown New Orleans in 1938. He was forty-nine at the time, so he started work at the store when he was sixteen.

Of course, there were many happier gatherings for the Krauss family. The Krauss Employees Benevolent Association held its first "fancy dress and masquerade ball" on Saturday, March 5, 1935. The ball, held at the Druids' Home on Camp Street, marked the fourteenth anniversary of the group. By 1939, the Association's Carnival celebration had evolved into a full tableau Bal Masqué. The Krauss Employees Dramatic Club named Leon Marks as King Phaeton I. The consort of the Son of Helios, Queen Thalia I, was Miss Thelma Bernard. Her maids were Misses Vivian Goeddertz, Marilyn Marks,

Lena Monteleone, Olga Ortega, Adele Sanchez and Beatrice Bongiavanni. The event was held at the Embassy Club.

The association held its annual outing for the eleventh year in 1936. The group and guests, totaling about five hundred, gathered in Mandeville, on the north shore of Lake Pontchartrain. Night baseball came to New Orleans in 1936, and the Commercial Athletic Association was well pleased to take part.

Ladies were able to get the "machineless permanent" from Zotos at the Krauss beauty parlor in the late 1930s. The *Zotos Hour of Charm* was broadcast on Sunday afternoons on WWL Radio. Krauss was able to piggyback on the company's advertising. The store also worked with other radio stations in town. In 1938, Krauss sponsored *Jean Abbey, Radio Shopper for Woman's Home Companion*, who discussed spring fashions on air on January 25.

America managed to keep the turmoil in Europe at a distance, but the Jewish community of New Orleans had observed the moves made by Adolf Hitler through the 1930s with more than passing interest. The pogrom against Jews in Germany that took place in November 1938 reverberated as far away as the United States. *Kristallnacht*, as the incident became known, heralded the horrors that were to come when war began.

6

Krauss at War

And now the company jumps when he plays reveille
He's the boogie woogie bugle boy of Company B
—the Andrews Sisters

The turmoil in Europe in 1939 was of interest to many, but it was business as usual in New Orleans. All-day parking cost shoppers who drove to Canal Street ten cents in the block behind the store. Works Progress Administration (WPA) projects in New Orleans created many jobs, stemming the tide of Depression-era unemployment. Among the federally funded projects that had a major impact in New Orleans were the Lake Pontchartrain seawall, which extended from West End to the Industrial Canal; Shushan Airport (Now New Orleans Lakefront Airport); and Tad Gormley Stadium in City Park, along with numerous other improvements to City Park. Men went to work on these projects, and their wives often went to work in the shops and stores on Canal Street. Krauss Co. Ltd. continued to offer their wares at low prices.

Another federal project that would have an effect on Krauss was the construction of the Lafitte Housing Project. The Housing Authority of New Orleans announced in the fall of 1939 that several low-cost housing developments would be constructed. The Lafitte development would replace the houses and other buildings of the old Storyville district with three-story brick apartment buildings. Lafitte was to be one of two housing developments exclusively for African American tenants. This housing

The Lafitte Housing complex now consists of new townhouses (*foreground*) and the older, WPA-built apartments from the 1940s. *Author photo.*

development would shape the neighborhood around Krauss for the fifty-seven remaining years of the store's existence. The Lafitte radically changed the dynamics of Treme. The ethnic makeup of the neighborhood shifted as African American families returned in numbers to Treme for the first time since Jim Crow.

The new development behind the store didn't change the business practices at Krauss. The store was already so committed to being a low-price leader, it was already the logical place for shoppers on a budget. White families living in the Iberville Project (on Orleans Avenue) as well black families in Lafitte were attracted to the store's basics. They could use the Krauss Club Plan to buy furniture and appliances, and the store's massive fabric department made it easier to keep the family clothed. Getting to the store was an easy walk for folks living in either development.

A public housing project behind the store did not stop Leon Heymann's plans for growing Krauss. By 1940, Heymann had acquired the property behind the store, in the 1200 block of Iberville. He began consulting with architects from Favrot & Reed to build a warehouse and service building in that block. The plans called for a connector to join the buildings together, over Iberville Street. Air conditioning and power distribution could be relocated to the new building, with ducts blowing cool air back into the store passing overhead via the connector. Stock could be transferred from the warehouse area to the store as well. Moving all the support services to a support building would open up a great deal of floor space for sales.

Such a move would require some serious redesign in the current store, though. To that end, Heymann sent his son, James (Jimmy); his brother-in-law, Leon Wolf; and an architect from Favrot & Reed on a road trip. Their mission was to check out how other stores were implementing air conditioning. They were also tasked with observing other aspects of department store operations. The plans came together over 1941, but the war put the expansion on hold for over ten years.

A more short-term modernization came to Krauss in 1940: new escalators. Even though the store installed an up-only escalator in 1923, Krauss continued to rely on elevators to move shoppers vertically through the five floors of retail space. That changed in 1940, when escalators that were used in the New York World's Fair from the previous year were installed.

The main structural features of the 1939 World's Fair were the Trylon and Perisphere. The Trylon was a spire-shaped 610-foot tower. The Perisphere was a spherical building, 180 feet in diameter, built next to the Trylon. The two were connected by what was billed as the longest escalator in the world at the time. In addition to that escalator, the Westinghouse company installed additional "moving stairways" (it couldn't use "escalator" since it was trademarked by Otis) in its pavilion.

All the structures of the World's Fair were intended to be temporary. Most of the site in Flushing Meadows, Queens, was razed after the fair closed. That meant there was a lot of surplus equipment available. Krauss negotiated to acquire the escalators in the Westinghouse pavilion. When they were installed at 1201 Canal Street, Krauss became the first store to have escalators going up and down. The art deco style and wood steps in the 1940 escalator were a fond experience for shoppers right up to the store's closure.

New Orleans moved forward in 1940. The port was coming back strong, after the Depression shut down so much foreign trade. The new Charity Hospital was fully open, caring for the sick of the city. The city had a public hospital since the 1730s. "Big Charity" was one of Huey Long's projects, conceived when he was governor of Louisiana and brought to fruition with federal funding he delivered as a U.S. senator. The hospital was integrated, accepting patients across the social and ethnic spectrum of the city. Such a large hospital was not only a boon to the construction business, but it

James "Jimmy" Heymann (*left*) and Hugo Kahn pose in front of the 1939-vintage escalator in the early 1970s. *Krauss Collection, University of New Orleans Earl K. Long Library.*

also became a steady, long-term employer. Hospitals naturally employ many people who support the doctors and nurses offering primary patient care. Many of those folks needed work clothes, uniforms that were inexpensive and easy to clean. The Krauss Uniform Department, essentially an extension of the store's other ready-to-wear departments, met these needs.

Once someone accepted employment at Charity Hospital, it was only a five-block walk over to Krauss to get work clothes. Since a large hospital attracts medical support businesses and offices to its neighborhood, uniform sales were solid business for the store.

The steamer *Capitol* continued to cruise the river in 1940, offering recreation and entertainment at affordable prices to Krauss employees. Traditional jazz music had evolved into the big band and swing sounds, but there was always good dance music. In addition to the steamboats, other clubs, like the Blue Room at the Roosevelt Hotel (three blocks down on Canal from Krauss), featured big bands regularly.

Visitors took in all aspects of the city, and the Creole French culture of New Orleans was still strong. In 1940, the *Atlantic* wrote:

> *French culture is tenacious. Its fierceness is equaled only by that of a Congressman clinging to his prerogative of putting his relatives on the federal payroll. Here we find France celebrated in streets called Dauphine, Toulouse, Bourbon, Burgundy, Ibervile, and Bienville. The Catholic religion is enshrined in street signs reading Ascension, Nuns, Piety, Religious, Assumption, and Annunciation. And if gods do not stroll the streets of New Orleans, mortals walk the streets of the gods: Urania, Melpomene,*

Krauss Uniform Department, 1943. *Krauss Collection, University of New Orleans Earl K. Long Library.*

Canal Street at night, 1941. *Krauss Collection, University of New Orleans Earl K. Long Library.*

> *Terpsichore, Clio, and Thalia. A shabby tribute is paid the memory of long departed first families by naming shabby streets in their honor: Choctaw, Teche, Natchez, Opelousas, and Tchoupitoulas.*

New Orleans worked its magic on locals and visitors alike. And like the locals, many visitors who stayed in Canal Street hotels made their way to Krauss for necessities as well as fripperies.

The Battle of Britain was of interest to New Orleans in the summer and fall of 1940. While the British were successful in holding off the Nazis, it was clear that they would not be able to maintain the defense of their country without outside help. FDR secured approval from Congress to begin sending weapons and supplies to the United Kingdom, under the Lend Lease program. Tanks, planes, jeeps, trucks and other supplies were manufactured in the United States and shipped across the Atlantic. New Orleans was still the second-largest port in the nation, so much of those goods went through the city. The war was strengthening the economy without Americans having to make serious sacrifices.

This situation changed on December 7, 1941, with the Japanese attack on U.S. military facilities in Hawaii. With the country formally at war with both Japan and Germany, productions of the necessities of war geared up dramatically. Before the war, Andrew Jackson Higgins owned a lumber business. He used his lumber to start a boat building company that sold inexpensive, flat-bottom wooden boats that were designed to navigate the bayous and access canals of south Louisiana to support oil drilling in the swamps. In 1938, Higgins Industries went to work on converting designs to support the U.S. Marine Corps. The final design, the Landing Craft Vehicle Personnel (LCVP), went into mass production at facilities along Bayou St. John and the New Basin Canal. The Higgins Boat helped win the war, in both Europe and the Pacific. In addition to the landing craft, Higgins Industries also manufactured Patrol-Torpedo (PT) boats for the navy, which were used in the Pacific. Consolidated Aircraft saw how easy it was for Higgins to test boats on Lake Pontchartrain. The company built a factory right on the lake, in Gentilly, to make PBY Catalina aircraft. The assembly line started blocks back and ended with a ramp where the finished seaplanes would float out into the lake. The boats and planes would then be brought down to the river and shipped overseas. Manufacturing was booming, and the Port of New Orleans was back to work.

Back to work meant families had more discretionary income to spend, but the war effort still limited many of those choices. Krauss came under fire from several manufacturers for fair trade practices, as the company sold products for below the pricing schedules set by the state. The corporate response was usually that since Krauss had no contracts with those companies, it was not bound by their pricing demands.

Spring and summer hats from the "French Room" in the millinery department were still hot items in the 1942, with half-price sales that summer. Krauss fabrics for dresses, graduation frocks and other purposes ranged from sixty-nine cents to two dollars a yard. Ready-to-wear dresses were also bringing in ladies looking to update their wardrobes. By the time the country had been at war for a full year, the store offered reversible coats, formal frocks and a large line of costume jewelry. The price was right at Krauss, and the customers loved it. Leon Wolf, store manager, told *Southwestern Retailer* magazine that business was up 12 percent from 1941 and that cash payments were up 26 percent.

The boom was welcome, but it came at a terribly high price. No doubt everyone looked long and hard to find a color photo of a marine that was lost on the second floor on Saturday, December 12, 1942, since families didn't know when their loved ones were coming home, if at all. The Krauss Department Store family offered themselves and their family members to the war effort. Jimmy Heymann became an officer in the U.S. Naval Reserve, which removed him from day-to-day operations at the store. Appliances'

Lieutenant Jimmy Heymann, USNR, holding his son, Jerry, 1944. *Krauss Collection, University of New Orleans Earl K. Long Library.*

Sig Warshauer enlisted in the navy in 1942 and was discharged after being commissioned as an officer in 1945. Luncheonette/cafeteria manager L.J. Theriot also chose the navy, cooking aboard ships. Andrew Gonzales, a navy carpenter's mate, was safer than many, crating and loading ammunition in Port Chicago, California.

The staff of Krauss held their collective breath in October 1942, when they learned that Norman Sarrat, the son of Comptroller Pete Sarrat, went missing on the fifth of that month. Lieutenant Sarrat was a navigator on a B-17 "Flying Fortress" in Europe. The Krauss employee newsletter, *What's Cooking?*, expressed the sentiments of many working at the store:

> *When one, who is close to us and as popular as Pete Sarrat has a tragic experience, we quickly come to the realization, that war is everything that Sherman said it was—It makes us realize when read in the papers that "ONLY five of our planes are missing", is a terrible loss. It means that 50 boys like Norman Sarrat, the Cream of our country are gone, and that 50 homes are crushed by this horrible war.*

Private First Class Siper Dikerson, stove truck helper, in the U.S. Army, 1944. *Krauss Collection, University of New Orleans Earl K. Long Library.*

What's Cooking? wasn't always this gloomy, though. The store also published periodic general-news editions of the newsletter. These editions contained news from around the city, as well as items specific to the store. These newsletters were cleared by military censors and then mailed to Krauss personnel around the world. It was a great way to keep their spirits up.

Heymann and Wolf were very focused on the contributions to the war effort they could make personally and on behalf of the store. Concern over security led to Leon Wolf implementing a "payroll stuffer" program. The idea was to include notes stuffed in with the employee pay envelopes that encouraged "Silence." The "stuffers" were four-page notes. The front cover opened with the text, "I pledge allegiance" accompanied by an illustration of an American flag, then continued, "and SILENCE about the war." Inside, the folder said:

"Allegiance to our flag is shared by all but a very few, BUT…SILENCE about the war is not as carefully maintained. You can do untold damage to our men (your loved ones) in service and our war effort by CARELESSLY TALKING ABOUT THE WAR."

The stuffer program was such a success, Wolf forwarded information and samples from the program to the Adjutant General's office of the War Department in June 1942. Wolf received a reply from the War Department, thanking him for the store's efforts. It also suggested he present the idea to the city's association of commerce so local stores and businesses could copy what Krauss was doing.

Security and silence weren't the only topics of payroll stuffers. Wolf also had stuffers printed up that encouraged employees to buy war bonds. He sent samples of these to the War Savings Program of the Treasury Department, which was very interested in the program.

Sale of war bonds was crucial to the ongoing effort. Krauss went further than just encouraging employees to buy bonds. Like New Orleans Public Service Inc. (NOPSI), the city's streetcar and bus operator, Wolf saw the

First-floor sales clerks Claire Lannes, Rosalie James and Dorothy Oechsle, on an outing at the Lakefront, 1943. *Krauss Collection, University of New Orleans Earl K. Long Library.*

store's delivery trucks as an opportunity to promote sale of bonds. He directed that the trucks be painted red, white and blue, with "BUY WAR BONDS NOW" displayed prominently on their sides. Like the red, white and blue streetcars that brought folks downtown in 1942–44, Krauss delivery trucks did their part.

The coverage area of those delivery trucks was scaled back by government regulations in an effort to save gas. The Office of Defense Transportation limited deliveries from retail stores to any one part of the city to only twice a week. Usually, Krauss trucks would deliver merchandise daily across the city. This regulation changed the delivery strategy. The delivery department divided the city into three sections and alternated deliveries between those sections. This meant there were some slow days for the delivery department, followed by a hectic one the next day. In addition to the delivery scheduling rules, the government specified that only items weighing five or more pounds or measuring sixty or more inches in girth were eligible for delivery. The managers of the department, Mike Montelepre, Louis Martinez and Simon Smith, kept tabs on the rules and their drivers accordingly.

Bowling became a much more popular pastime in the 1940s, to the point where the ladies of Krauss formed an in-house bowling league in 1942. The teams were the Pop-Hys, named for "Pop" Heymann; the Maxies for Max Krauss; the Fritzerettes for Fritz Krauss; the Jim-Jams for Jimmy Heymann; the Wolferettes for Leon Wolf; and the Gar-fins for Harry Garfinkle. The mother-daughter combo of Hilda Hennessey (Gar-Fins) and Gloria

Delivery driver Frank Coffey with his truck in 1943. *Krauss Collection, University of New Orleans Earl K. Long Library*.

Hennessey Durbin (Fritzerettes) captained their respective teams, and the competition was reported to be intense.

Anxiety over the fates of loved ones overseas didn't improve in 1943. Life went on, as "full fashion rayon hose" were sixty-nine cents a pair. Sam Krauss spent the first half of 1943 recovering from a hit-and-run auto accident in October 1942. A young man ran a stop sign, hitting Krauss. While his injuries were not life-threatening, the hard collision took its toll on the older man. The driver fled the scene but was later caught. By the time the driver had been sentenced to sixty days in jail, Krauss had fully recovered.

Leather and rubber continued to be rationed items, so the Krauss Shoe Repair Shop was quite busy throughout the war years. In addition to standard repair work designed to keep shoes going a bit longer, the shop offered a whitening process to make last year's white shoes look new for the spring and summer. The store came under fire from Pepsodent in 1942 for selling items at prices lower than the corporate schedule; in 1943, Mennen and Bristol-Meyers both sued Krauss over the same issue.

The payroll stuffers program continued at Krauss, and both store personnel and managers were some of the top war bond purchasers in New Orleans. Since Leon Heymann purchased the most war bonds in the Treasury Department's "Christmas in July" sale in 1943, he could designate a sponsor to christen a Delta Shipbuilding Company ship, the SS *Reginald A. Fessenden*, on August 26, 1943. Heymann chose Mary Gundof, a Krauss employee who lived in Mid City, since her son was a private in the U.S. Army. Mrs. Gundof was joined on the platform that day by Anna Mae Falcon, Gloria Durbin, Mable LeBlanc, Flo Rauch and Una Toups. These ladies were all also Krauss employees. Their husbands were serving in various capacities overseas.

Nationwide, production of communications equipment for the war effort was down 3 percent in the summer of 1943. The massive need for radios and other electronic equipment was visible by the empty shelves in Krauss's radio department. Stocks of necessities such as furniture and bedding were still solid, and the "carrying charge" for credit payment was still low.

The up-and-down escalators were still a new novelty at Krauss in 1943, and the store promoted their use and convenience almost daily. It's no surprise that there were occasional escalator-related injuries, like when Roque Marcade, age three, got his hand caught on the escalator at the second-floor landing. Harry Garfinkle, the second-floor manager, reacted immediately, clearing the child away. He was taken to the hospital for treatment of lacerations. Shopping went on.

Unidentified group of sales clerks promoting war bonds in 1943. *Krauss Collection, University of New Orleans Earl K. Long Library.*

Operation Overlord, the invasion of France, was well underway when Krauss employees woke up and went to work on June 6, 1944. The usual banter as everyone prepared for the workday was quite subdued. A general assembly of employees was called for 9:30 a.m. Management directed employees to focus on the sales of war bonds, as well as taking time to donate blood to the Red Cross. All employees were encouraged to donate blood at the blood bank, which was located just down the street at 123 Carondelet. Krauss's quota in June 1944 was twenty-five new donors. *What's Cooking?* was pleased to report that Gladys Soigner, Pearl Pusateri, L. Gulino, Mollie Wald, Edith Holt, Nina Richards, Mrs. R.C. Weixel and Mal Cohen were in that number. Elizabeth Carrigan led those assembled in the singing of "The Star-Spangled Banner."

A 1945 ad in the *New Orleans States* for "non-rationed" shoes. *Krauss Collection, University of New Orleans Earl K. Long Library.*

There was a minute of silent prayer, and the assembly disbanded, as everyone took to the sales floor.

Krauss regularly sponsored radio programs throughout the 1940s. During the war years, one of these programs was a "Blue Network" program featuring war correspondent Martin Agronsky, who presented a fifteen-minute daily update every morning in 1944. Summer Slack Suits were $2.95 each, and Women's Printed House Coats were $1.95 that summer. The store's Shoe Department occasionally acquired overstock lots from manufacturers and other retail chains, so Krauss was offered "ration-free" shoes, if ladies didn't mind the limited selection in sizes and styles. Shoppers were encouraged to "buy another war bond" when they bought "non-rationed" casual shoes and sandals in March 1945.

The men of Krauss serving overseas didn't return home immediately after V-E Day and V-J Day. Jimmy Heymann was back at the store in the fall of 1945, discharged from the U.S. Naval Reserve. On May 25, 1945, Heymann received a citation for "meritorious achievement in the performance of outstanding service as Officer in Charge, LCI(L) Loading and Servicing Detail, Lambert's Point, Norfolk, Virginia, Amphibious Training Command, United States Atlantic Fleet, from August, 1944 to May, 1945." He immediately assumed greater responsibility at Krauss, allowing his father to scale back his work schedule. Others didn't get back until 1946, when they began in earnest to bring various store departments back to where they were before the war limited the merchandise they could acquire. For example, it would be months before former Ensign Sig Warshauer, now the electrical appliances manager, would be able to re-stock the store's radio product line. When he returned from the navy, all that remained were two sample units.

Still, the war was over, and everyone at Krauss was excited to get their loved ones back home, as the country settled back into peacetime.

7

Expansion and Boom

Tipitina tra la la la
Whoa la la la-ah tra la la la
Tipitina, hoola malla walla dalla
Tra ma ti na na
—*Professor Longhair, "Tipitina"*

When Otis Crier and George Bullock returned home after their four-year enlistment terms in the U.S. Army, the Krauss Delivery Department was glad to have them back. As the men and women who fought the war returned home, they began to look for places of their own to live. They left home as teenagers and returned as adults, ready to continue their education and start families. Krauss was more than happy to be part of that process, selling them the things necessary to keep the modern family of 1946 moving.

With the store settling into peacetime, things that were put on hold in 1942 were front and center again, from that new bedroom set the couple in Treme wanted to the Krauss annual Carnival Bal Masqué. The 1946 Bal Masqué was held on February 2, 1946. Knowing that many former kings and queens of Carnival balls did not have strong emotional attachments to the regalia they used on their night in the spotlight, the ball committee advertised to buy crowns and scepters for their king and queen. The response to the ad was excellent, and the committee purchased a lovely set. Carrie DePaoli reigned as queen, with Jake Mesinger as her consort. Unlike prewar balls, the 1946 affair was sponsored by Krauss

John Duthu and Nathan Moskowitz returned to work in the Shoe Department in the fall of 1945. *Krauss Collection, University of New Orleans Earl K. Long Library.*

management, rather than the employees' association. The Municipal Auditorium, just down the street from the store, was the venue, and about one thousand guests attended. Russ Papalia & His Orchestra provided the music, and the krewe danced until two o'clock in the morning.

Carnival at Krauss broke new ground in 1948 when African American employees organized and held their first Bal Masqué. The black employees of the store voted for a queen and four maids. Leon Heymann supervised the ballot-counting. Rose Mary Pierre of the will-call department (and daughter of head porter Eddie Pierre) was chosen queen. Her maids were Ruth Williams, Adelaide Bertrand, Bernadette Mims and Bernadine Villavosa. The king was Otis Crier, and his dukes were Gilmore Alexander, Arthur Nash, Leon Williams and Nathaniel Patterson. The venue for the ball was Dillard University, and it was held on January 28, 1948. While many jobs were not available to black people at the time, Krauss nonetheless hired many maids, porters, truck drivers, warehousemen, elevator operators and cooks. The staff reflected the store's neighborhood, Treme, as much as a segregated workforce could.

Krauss Employees Carnival Ball, 1946. Jake Mesinger is the king; Carrie DePaoli is the queen. *Krauss Collection, University of New Orleans Earl K. Long Library.*

In the larger community, changes in the public transit system were afoot. Many of the city's streetcar lines were converted to buses. The War Department did not permit NOPSI to discontinue streetcar operations during the war because rubber was an important commodity for military use and was rationed. When these restrictions were lifted, the transit operator replaced streetcars with bus service. By 1948, the only lines still operating streetcars were St. Charles Avenue and Canal Street. The corner of Canal and Rampart was still an active transit interchange, in spite of this conversion. Since that was just a block down from the train station and Krauss, things were still quite busy in front of the store.

The Krauss Bowlerettes continued their intramural league but also mustered a team for the Commercial Athletic Association's women's league. The Krauss ladies competed against teams from U.S. Engineers, Maison Blanche, D.H. Holmes, Marks Issacs and Godchaux's, in 1947. The teams in the Bowlerette league, which played regularly at Metropolitan Lanes, were the Moppers, Toppers, Floppers and Whoppers. The men of Krauss also took to the lanes in the C.A.A., battling Higgins Industries, Regal Brewing, the *Times-Picayune* newspaper, Dixie Brewing, U.S. Engineers, Celotex, D.H. Holmes, the Red Cross and Godchaux's.

Many Krauss employees vacationed out of town in the years after the war, since wartime rationing of gas and tires had been lifted. *What's Cooking?*

reported that Ike Layman and Harry Strasburger went to New York City and William H. Richardson visited family in Lafayette and Dallas, but Marie Guzzardo didn't get much farther than Mandeville. "Uncle Charlie" of the shipping department didn't leave town but spent a lot of his free time in movie theaters.

The number of young families looking to purchase their own homes grew in the late 1940s. A number of WPA projects before the war involved street paving and other development in Lakeview and Gentilly. Contractors built subdivisions in both neighborhoods, creating a housing boom. Krauss worked with the Housing Authority of New Orleans (HANO) to exhibit apartments in housing projects that were fully furnished with items from the store. As more and more shoppers looked to upgrade their kitchens, dining rooms and bedrooms, Krauss was there with a wide selection of furniture and appliances. "Do you have your 'CHARGA PLATE'?" became a common refrain among Krauss sales clerks, as the store began issue credit cards to customers.

Mal Cohen, children's and dress buyer, and Josie Bruno, artist, join advertising manager Ed Schwartz in his office to plan print ads, 1943. *Krauss Collection, University of New Orleans Earl K. Long Library.*

Retailers began to eye the possibilities of moving out from Canal Street to service these growing areas. Maison Blanche was the first of the city's department stores to expand out from Canal Street, opening up a store at Carrollton and Tulane Avenues in Mid City and a second store on Frenchmen Street and Gentilly Road, just off of Elysian Fields Avenue, in Gentilly. Other stores began to consider locations outside the Central Business District as well, but the Heymanns remained firm. They stuck to Canal Street and Faubourg Treme.

Indeed, the expansion of Krauss involved moving into the next block, not into new neighborhoods. Heymann's expansion plan from 1940 was ready to be implemented. On March 13, 1950, Leon Heymann announced that R.P. Farnsworth Company Inc. had been selected to build the service building that would occupy the block on Basin Street, from Iberville Street back to Bienville Street. The architectural firm of Favrot & Livaudais designed the original 1940 expansion and re-joined the project in 1950. This was perfectly logical; in 1909, the firm built Leon Heymann's store in Houma and enjoyed a good relationship with him since then.

By moving a number of aspects of physical plant support to the 180,000-square-foot service building, 95,000 square feet of space in the store would be freed up and turned into retail sales space. Employees were told they could look forward to expanded and upgraded recreational space at the back of the store upon the new building's completion.

The new building was nearing completion when Leon and Thekla Heymann celebrated their forty-fifth wedding anniversary that June. Leon Wolf presented the couple with a clipping from the *New Orleans Times-Democrat*'s edition on June 17, 1906, describing the wedding.

Once the connector between the store building and the service building was complete and the new building's freight elevators became operational, stock rooms in the store building were moved one block back. Jimmy Heymann was the go-to man on the new building project, while Leon Wolf remained superintendent of Krauss. Several departments were shuffled around in the store, taking advantage of all that freed-up space. The Furniture Department moved to the fifth floor and Sporting Goods to the fourth floor, and the store began looking at creating a Jewelry Department on the first floor. The store's offices, switchboard and Credit Department also moved to the fifth floor. The expansion in space for the "Club Plan" and "Time Pay" operations meant that Krauss would begin selling everything in the store on credit, not just larger purchases such as furniture and appliances.

Unidentified Krauss employees observe the groundbreaking on the 1950 expansion project. *Krauss Collection, University of New Orleans Earl K. Long Library.*

The connector linking the main store with the Iberville Street Service Building still exists at the 1201 Canal Condominiums. *Author's collection.*

The Delivery Department moved to the service building, which had four truck bays on the Basin Street side. Keep in mind that the Southern Railway passenger terminal was still located on Basin Street, making that a busy commercial area and not the wide neutral ground it is today. The original 1940 plan for the service building called for moving the air conditioning plant out of the store building, pumping the cool air back to the store through the connector over Iberville Street. This was implemented, but ten years made an incredible difference in the air conditioning equipment, making it some of the most modern in the city.

The business boom of the late 1940s and early 1950s was incredible, but store management still saw no reason to extend the store's hours beyond 6:00 p.m. in the evening. Every fall, the store would run newspaper ads, reminding shoppers that Krauss's hours were 9:45 a.m. to 6:00 p.m., even as Christmas approached, so employees could "get home at a reasonable hour."

With the store's regular operations in the capable hands of Leon Wolf and Jimmy Heymann, Leon Heymann was able to focus on some of the other projects in the community that were important to him. In 1951, the Leon Heymann Foundation financed and constructed a Colored Home for the Incurables, on Bordeaux Street, Uptown. This facility gave African

Americans a place where chronically ill family members could receive care similar to the (white) Home for the Incurables, farther uptown, on Henry Clay Avenue. The home opened in June 1952.

Another significant feature expanded with the construction of the service building was the store's infirmary. The infirmary, staffed by a nurse, with a doctor on-call, had been a Krauss employee benefit for decades, and the 1950 expansion allowed the infirmary to grow. The new infirmary consisted of a reception area, two examining rooms and four "quiet rooms" where employees feeling a bit under the weather could sit and rest for a while before returning to the sales floor. The store also increased the availability of a doctor on the premises. By the opening of the expanded infirmary, a doctor was available to employees for a couple hours each weekday. Leon Heymann liked to regularly point out the practicality of the infirmary and how it occasionally benefitted shoppers as well as staff. In addition to the infirmary, the company covered all the expenses of a Blue Cross health plan for employees. Other employee benefits were a lending library consisting of over 1,200 titles and a pension plan.

Krauss boasted it was "rarin' to go!" in the *Times-Picayune* on New Year's Day 1952. The ad featured an aerial view of the 8.5-acre store and service building. It also noted the new parking lots constructed nearby. As always, the store touted its simplicity and low prices.

The "CHARGA PLATE" system was gaining in popularity, but the old-style "coupon" system was upgraded to what Leon Wolf called the "Certificate Plan" in November 1952. The shopper would buy a minimum of 24 $1 certificates and pay for them over six months. The certificates could then be used in any department in the store. No doubt, some of those certificates were used to purchase "Whittendon" Blanket Robes for ladies, on sale for $2.95.

Unlike their competitors down the street, Maison Blanche, Krauss did not have a signature holiday character, like MB did with "Mister Bingle." That sort of promotion did not fit into Heymann's business model. The store did hire a Santa Claus, who greeted children in the fourth-floor toy department. The kind of news Heymann and Krauss preferred to make was the distribution of $125,000 in bonus checks in December 1952. Heymann always believed that word-of-mouth promotion from happy employees was his best asset.

Not having a unique Christmas character didn't mean Krauss had boring window displays. The store's display manager, J. Phil Preddy, was an excellent artist with an eye for what would attract the attention of folks

Christmas display mural by J. Phil Preddy, 1952. *Krauss Collection, University of New Orleans Earl K. Long Library.*

walking down Canal Street. The Sugar Bowl was an important event on the tourism calendar of New Orleans, and the week between Christmas and New Year's was filled with pre-game activity. In the 1950s, Preddy would create window displays for Krauss made of blocks of sugar. He would assemble and sculpt large blocks of sugar, provided to him by local sugar companies. He discovered that he could lightly paint the blocks, and a Krauss tradition was born.

The *Times-Picayune's* Sunday magazine, the *Dixie Roto*, did a feature on Preddy in the run-up to the 1953 Sugar Bowl, which matched Ole Miss against Georgia Tech. Georgia Tech won the game and the national championship that season. Preddy created thirty-six action figures of players from both teams. They joined a replica of Tulane Stadium (home of the Sugar Bowl) originally created by Preddy for the 1952 game that was also carved from sugar blocks. Phil Preddy was more than just a window dresser. In his time away from the store, one of Preddy's projects/hobbies was to paint murals of the Jordan River in the baptisteries of churches in the region. By the end of 1952, he had painted forty-four of these murals.

Preddy painted his largest and arguably best-remembered mural in 1953. The canvas was located on the front of Krauss Department Store, at 1201 Canal Street. The mural featured the store, as viewed from Basin Street. It was a timeline of the various expansions, from the original Fellman building in 1903 and the 1911, 1923, 1927 and 1952 expansions. The occasion was the fiftieth anniversary of the store's opening. Krauss celebrated the anniversary throughout 1953. The local press made a big deal out of it in April. The *Times-Picayune* did a feature on the history of the store and Leon Heymann on April 19. Heymann, as was his wont, spent more time in the interview showing off the behind-the-scenes facilities for employees than the sale floors themselves. When the reporter asked him to pose for a picture to accompany the interview, he declined, as he always did. The article explains: "His modesty is indicated in his steadfast refusal to allow his picture to be taken for publication in the newspapers and he has consistently kept himself out of the public limelight. When asked in this interview for permission to take his picture, he emphatically said: 'You'll see my picture in the newspapers when I die.' Then, after a moment's reflection, 'Maybe.'" Heymann's photo ended up in the local papers twice in the 1950s. In 1956, on the occasion of his seventy-fifth birthday, he posed for a photo with his wife, daughter May and her husband, Leon

Fiftieth anniversary display mural by J. Phil Preddy, 1953. *Krauss Collection, University of New Orleans Earl K. Long Library.*

Leon Heymann (*right*) receives the fifth annual Weiss Brotherhood Award from C.C. Walther, Protestant co-chairman of the New Orleans Chapter of the National Conference of Christians and Jews, November 1958. *Krauss Collection, University of New Orleans Earl K. Long Library.*

Wolf. In 1958, his photograph was published a second time, when he was named the recipient of the Weiss Award.

In addition to the giant mural on the front of the store, Preddy and his display shop created one of the most memorable display features in the history of the store. A frame and railing was installed above the marquee on the front of the store, facing Canal Street. They then cut letters from plywood, six feet tall, painted them white and installed waterproofed light bulbs into each letter. With sixty-seven different letters, numerals and symbols, Preddy turned the front of the store into a giant advertisement. During the fiftieth anniversary sale, the sign was regularly changed: "50-Cent Day," "Dollar Day" and other promotions were featured. The display even made the October issue of *LIFE* magazine in 1953, as Krauss welcomed director-producer Josh Logan back to Louisiana. Logan presented an off-Broadway opening of his new comedy, *Kind Sir*, featuring Mary Martin (*South Pacific*).

"WELCOME JOSH LOGAN & KIND SIR" was the message in lights on the front of Krauss in October 1953. *Krauss Collection, University of New Orleans Earl K. Long Library.*

Other messages on the big sign were "Welcome Ike and Ambassadors," on a presidential visit, as well as promotion of the United Fund's annual drive that fall. When Terminal Station was demolished, the sign was extended onto the Basin Street side of the store. Once Wolf and Preddy approved a message for the sign, it took the porters about three hours to put that message up.

The semi-tropical weather of New Orleans made the roll-out of a refrigerator/freezer from Servel with an automatic ice maker a big deal in February 1952. Hopefully, some of the Krauss employees playing in the CAA softball leagues that summer were able to buy them, so they could come home to ice-cold refreshments after the games.

In its fiftieth year, the management team at Krauss was led by Leon Heymann as president. Max Krauss was vice-president, with Jimmy Heymann as secretary and Leon Wolf, superintendent and treasurer. The anniversary year was bittersweet, however; Frederick "Fritz" Krauss, one of the founding Krauss brothers, passed away on April 15.

Wrangler Jeans were one of the promotions featured on the big sign in 1954, as part of a product promotion. Wrangler made a pair of jeans from forty-two mink skins for the front display. They were modeled regularly by Mickey Freibert and were on sale for $3,500.

Canal Street and Faubourg Treme experienced some major changes in the mid- to late 1950s. Mayor deLesseps Story "Chep" Morrison's

Miss Mickey Friebert models a pair of mink jeans as part of a Wrangler Jeans promotion, 1954. *Krauss Collection, University of New Orleans Earl K. Long Library.*

dream of a single, unified, railroad passenger terminal for the city became reality in 1954. The city opened the Union Passenger Terminal on Loyola Avenue, replacing the Illinois Central Union Station. Morrison ordered the other passenger terminals demolished. This included Terminal Station on Canal and Basin Streets, right next to Krauss. When the station was demolished, shoppers walking up Canal Street had an unobstructed view of Krauss along Basin Street for the first time since 1908. With the train station and the tracks behind it gone, Basin Street was converted into a four-lane boulevard, connecting Canal Street with the Municipal Auditorium. The neutral ground on Basin Street became home to a several monuments, with a statue of Simon Bolivar front and center on Canal Street. The city installed mercury vapor lamps along Basin. When the work was complete, Leon Wolf stood next to Mayor Morrison, on Thursday, May 19, 1955, as he pulled the switch to light up Basin for the first time.

Changes in the public transit system in the late 1940s and early '50s led the city to embark on a beautification program for Canal Street in 1957. By that time, the only streetcar lines left in New Orleans were the Canal Street and St. Charles Avenue lines. The four-track main line going down Canal Street in the CBD was no longer necessary. The city pulled up the two outside tracks along Canal, leaving just the two middle tracks and one block of the outside track on the inbound side (heading toward the river). That outside section allowed streetcars running on the St. Charles line to come to Canal Street on Carondelet Street, turn onto Canal for a block and turn onto St. Charles Avenue for the outbound run. The width of the neutral ground was reduced, creating a third automobile lane on either side.

Jimmy Heymann announced that Krauss would build a seven-story parking garage on Iberville and North Liberty Streets, just behind the store. The structure cost $500,000 and could accommodate 350 to 375 cars. This was a dramatic increase in store-owned parking; while there were a number of parking lots around Basin and North Rampart Streets, the store's lot could only park 90 cars.

In 1958, Krauss not only had a Santa in the Toy Department, but the store also sold Santa suits for customers to wear to their own holiday parties. Krauss also participated in a Christmas Parade on Canal Street on November 8, 1958. Sponsored by Downtown Merchants Inc., the parade began at 9:00 a.m. at Canal Street and Claiborne Avenue. The floats went down the uptown side of Canal, turned at Camp and went up the downtown side of Canal, passing Krauss just before disbanding on Claiborne. The parade featured large balloons, several over one hundred feet in length. Girls on the floats threw trinkets to the parade-goers in true Mardi Gras style. The parade also featured bands from Alcee Fortier, Warren Easton and Francis T. Nichols High Schools.

Krauss closed its doors for the day on December 18, 1959, to mark the passing of one of its founders, Max Krauss. He was the last brother, survived by three sisters.

Max Krauss, the last surviving founder of Krauss Department Store, at his desk in 1953. He passed away in 1959. *Krauss Collection, University of New Orleans Earl K. Long Library.*

After a successful "Community Bargain Days" promotion in February 1960, Krauss made a significant change in management structure to start the 1960s. In August, Leon Heymann brought in Paul McWilliams as general merchandise manager. It marked the first time in Heymann's tenure as president that a non-member of his family occupied a place in senior management.

An ad in the *Times-Picayune* on October 14, 1961, reminded shoppers that their original, metal CHARGA PLATE cards were still valid at the store, even though Krauss was switching to plastic credit cards. The store opened a Book Department on the first mezzanine in 1961, which was very popular by the time of the store's anniversary the following year. Three-piece dress suits for ladies were $10.98 in the fall holiday season.

Krauss received a major loss in January 1963, when its president, Leon Heymann, passed away on January 6. The store closed the next day, as Jimmy Heymann assumed the presidency of the company. Leon had been the company's president for over forty years, and the corporation's directors were restructured after his death. Jimmy Heymann became president of Krauss, with Leon Wolf becoming vice-president. Jimmy's sister May and his wife, Janice, became secretary and treasurer, respectively. A year later, Leon Wolf passed away, on January 14, 1964, at the age of sixty-five. Thekla Krauss Heymann passed away on April 7, 1964. Mrs. Heymann had been living with her daughter and son-in-law on Third Street at the time of her death.

The store kept going strong despite the passing of Wolf and the Heymanns. Jimmy Heymann was in full control and supervised improvements to the first-floor retail area, as well as the installation of new display windows in the front of the store. These improvements were in place for the store's sixty-second anniversary sale in April 1965.

That anniversary in 1965 was the first one in which streetcars did not pass in front of Krauss. On May 31, 1964, NOPSI discontinued streetcar operations on the Canal line. The streetcars were replaced with brand-new, air-conditioned buses. The tracks running the 4.3-mile length of Canal Street were ripped up. In the CBD, buses ran in the neutral ground. This change was hailed as a progressive one at the time. NOPSI operated express bus lines out to Lakeview so that commuters could ride from their homes directly into the CBD without transferring to the streetcar at head of Canal Street. As with every other transit change in the history of the store, Canal Street, between Rampart and Basin Streets, continued to be a hub of activity.

In 1967, Jimmy Heymann made major changes to the structure of Krauss Company Inc. It was clear that Heymann's son, Jerry, did not have an interest in the family business, so he chose directors from outside the family for the first time since his father bought out Leon Fellman. Jimmy and his wife elected Edward Bronston as executive vice-president. Paul McWilliams became vice-president for merchandising. Ludwig Behr became vice-president and manager of the store's New York office.

The fourth newcomer to the store was Hugo Kahn of Omaha, Nebraska. A certified public accountant, Kahn became vice-president and controller. The store's Canal Street competitors had long expanded out in the city and suburbs, and D.H. Holmes was the primary anchor of Lakeside Shopping Center in Metairie. Jimmy put together a strong team that would lead Krauss into the era of shopping malls.

8

Fabrics, Foundations and Food

Every year, at Carnival Time, we make a New Suit…
—the Wild Magnolias

Fabrics

It's difficult to point to one or two specific things that a store occupying 8.5 acres of downtown New Orleans carried as specialties or signature items. Still, if one were to say Krauss was known for selling this or that, most shoppers would point out the Fabric and Lingerie Departments.

Fabrics by the yard and the accessories needed to turn that fabric into clothing were some of the most common items sold by dry goods stores in the late 1800s. When retailers expanded their merchandise by opening department stores, naturally their fabric departments were still one of the big moneymakers.

Simply having an extensive Fabric Department wasn't good enough for Krauss. Those fabrics had to be for sale at the lowest prices possible. Within a month of its opening, the store's first ten-cent sale offered fabrics that normally sold for twenty-five cents a yard at ten cents per yard. Of course, accessories, such as "extra-large pearl buttons" were sold, two dozen on a card for twenty-five cents, discounted for the sale.

The Creoles of Treme and the ladies of Storyville, as well as women from all over town, knew Krauss was their go-to for their next dress or the curtains for their new home. The store had a seamstress shop that could turn those

Krauss newspaper ad, 1915. Ten-cents sales were a regular promotion for the store, 1915–25. *New Orleans Public Library.*

bolts of cotton, silk and lace, along with cards of buttons and zippers, into suits, dresses and gowns. Over the years, Leon Heymann would regularly use store-sponsored sewing classes as an example of the sort of in-store promotion he liked. From the Krauss perspective, these were big wins. Women learned a skill that required raw materials that could all be purchased at the store. Additionally, because Krauss was a department store, rather than simply a dry goods shop, it sold sewing machines. The various Krauss credit/payment plans enabled the would-be seamstress to purchase her sewing machine on reasonable terms. These sewing seminars continued long after Heymann passed away. In February 1984, the store held a seminar on "taking your measurements and choosing your pattern size."

The Fabric Department did not just carry material used for clothing. Krauss was also a great source for curtains and drapes. Customers could buy the material and make their own curtains or have them made by the store. Many of the city's better restaurants would come to Krauss for their curtains.

After World War II, ready-to-wear sales skyrocketed, as more women entered the workforce during the war years and stayed there. Krauss was still the downtown leader in fabric sales. In the 1970s, Krauss partnered with Vogue Patterns, holding events for seamstresses. When Edith Head of *Vogue* held a show in the Louisiana Superdome in 1979, Krauss sponsored the event. Head appeared at the store on December 1, 1979, to autograph patterns. Shoppers could purchase not only the *Vogue* patterns but also the American silks used to make the dresses exhibited at the fashion show.

Whimsy was just as important as practical when it came to fabric purchases in New Orleans. The city's annual Carnival celebration required various changes of clothing and costumes. From debutantes to Krauss employees themselves, women required gowns for the numerous balls held each winter. Debutantes had interesting needs. The "old-line" Carnival krewes were not just social gatherings but also debutante cotillions, where the daughters of influential families in New Orleans formally presented their daughters to society. It was quite possible that a young woman might be a maid in two

Right: A 1931 newspaper ad for Modernage sewing machines. *Krauss Collection, University of New Orleans Earl K. Long Library.*

Below: Fabric Department insert, mailed out with charge account statements, 1981. *Krauss Collection, University of New Orleans Earl K. Long Library.*

or three balls during her debutante season. The standard dress for the Bal Masqué as a maid was a long, white gown. It would be costly to buy multiple ready-to-wear gowns that would likely have to be tailored anyway. The young woman could purchase a pattern with options for multiple necklines, then either a relative would sew the gown or a seamstress would be hired.

In the 1980s, Krauss held an annual Fabric Fair in the Fall. In September 1985, the Fabric Department buyer/manager, Jay Klein, was proud to show off his extensive stock of Ultrasuede—thirty different colors, selling at thirty-five dollars per yard. Krauss sold fabrics that had all sorts of potential for masking for Carnival: sequined material, velvets, jacquard, all at reasonable prices. No doubt many of the contestants in the Bourbon Street Awards, the incredibly popular costume contest held annually since 1967, shopped at Krauss. Every year, dozens of men create elaborate costumes and parade them on a boxing ring–style stage erected at the intersection of Bourbon and Dumaine Streets in the French Quarter, "all on a Mardi Gras Day." Competing at the level of the Bourbon Street Awards requires a lot of skill and imagination, and Krauss was a wonderful source of raw materials.

Gay men aren't the only ones who make elaborate Carnival costumes. Every year, the black Mardi Gras Indian tribes labor long and hard to make a "new suit of pretty" to display on Mardi Gras Day. The Indian costumes require a massive amount of fabric and accessories. Many of the Indians are working-class men. While they are willing to sacrifice to pay for that "new suit," value was important. Say "value" to a New Orleans shopper, and "Krauss" came to mind. The Fabric Department understood the needs of the debutante, the drag queen and the Mardi Gras Indian in a way that no clerk in a national chain fabric store ever would.

Foundations

Krauss is gone,
So you can't try on,
No queen-size lingerie
—Benny "Grunch" Anton, "Ain't Dere No More"

The subject of a lady's foundations has been a touchy one for generations. Long before the days of the international chain stores selling lingerie, Krauss addressed this delicate need with the attention and discretion New Orleans'

Krauss credit card. This style was used from the 1970s to the 1990s. *Krauss Collection, University of New Orleans Earl K. Long Library.*

women desired. From the beginning, Krauss had a fully stocked lingerie department. There were values galore, such as a wide range of "Dainty Undermuslins," brassieres, corsets, chemises and drawers on sale in April 1912. In 1921, the bargains were on women's fleece-lined underwear, regularly $1.00, on sale for $0.59 in January 1921. Rubber "self-reducing" bras were on sale in 1924 for $1.25 each.

In 1951, *What's Cooking?* boasted of the expertise of the corset section of the Foundations Department. Corset buyer Virginia Rhodes, Louise Lecorgne, Bertha Hinderling and Rosalie Toll all had years of experience assisting women to get the perfect fit. The newsletter also lauded the expertise and good judgment of Dollie Gerson, negligee saleswoman in the Lingerie Department.

In the 1980s and 1990s, Krauss relied heavily on inserts included with the customer's credit card bill to advertise and promote lingerie. By this point, so many folks had moved out to the suburbs, the store looked for innovative ways to keep customers. Women regularly bought the same brand and style of bra and/or girdle, so offering them the option of mail-order was a way to keep their business. In 1991, ladies could buy an Exquisite Form long-line bra for fourteen dollars, plus sales tax and a three-dollar shipping charge. All they had to do was mail back the insert with their personal info and account number.

What was most important about these intimate purchases was that Krauss sales clerks were on hand to assist and advise the shopper. Mothers who didn't quite know how to deal with their preteen daughters' needs could go to Krauss, and the ladies working on the second floor would take the girl in hand and get her foundations settled. The personal touch kept women coming back for generations, as styles and the technology behind bras and girdles evolved.

FOOD

Red beans and rice for a quarter
You can see her almost any day
singing voulez vous
—Steely Dan, "Pearl of the Quarter"

Lunchtime was always easy to manage at the small dry goods stores of lower Canal Street. The staff ran out for something, time permitting. As Shwartz, Fellman and the Krauss brothers opened their department stores, however, the notion of "run out for something" became more and more complicated. This was especially true for Krauss, being farthest away from the lunch places in the Vieux Carré and the CBD. Krauss added an employee lunchroom in the 1911 expansion. It was located on the third floor. Employees could bring something from home or go out, pick up lunch and eat it back at the store. A couple years later, Leopold Krauss had a kitchen and dining room built on the store's fifth floor.

The in-store dining facilities were considered important by Krauss management because they enabled employees to eat lunch and get back to work as quickly as possible. Because of Jim Crow laws, a single kitchen serviced both the white and black dining rooms. Mamie Toekle, looking back in 1953, remembered that the price of lunch in the original dining room was fifteen cents, and seconds on dishes such as spaghetti and meatballs or gumbo were free. The employee dining room and, later, the expanded cafeteria, which opened after the service building was constructed in 1952, were operated on a nonprofit basis to keep the cost to employees at a bare minimum. When Margaret Allen came over to Krauss from Solari's in 1946, some of the lunches she offered included oyster soup, salads, pork chops, spareribs and gumbo.

Seaman's Cook Second Class L.J. Theriot, in the U.S. Navy, 1944. Theriot was the Luncheonette/Cafeteria manager before the war. *Krauss Collection, University of New Orleans Earl K. Long Library*.

The fifth-floor kitchen kept employees fed throughout the 1920s. In 1931, Leon Heymann expanded the store's food service to customers, opening a soda fountain and luncheonette on the first mezzanine. The fifth-floor kitchen provided "pot cooking" dishes such as gumbo, étoufée, spaghetti and meatballs and so on to the luncheonette. Sandwiches, ice cream treats and soft drinks were served directly from the behind the diner counter. Breakfast was served from store opening until noon. On the morning of October 20, 1943, Krauss superintendent Leon Wolf went up to the luncheonette to find two jovial couples. Sergeant Second Class John Dombeck and his wife of thirty minutes had come to Krauss straight from their wedding ceremony at Sacred Heart Catholic Church, farther up Canal Street. They were joined by Mrs. Walter Letter and Edward E. Wistrovski, who had come down from Menosha, Wisconsin, to be the Dombecks' matron of honor and best man. After greeting the happy couple and their guests, Wolf treated the Dombecks to a free portrait from the store's photo studio.

Mrs. Margaret Allen took over the Krauss food service operations in 1950. *Krauss Collection, University of New Orleans Earl K. Long Library.*

With the addition of the service building in 1952, the food services at the store were greatly expanded. The employee and executive dining rooms got a complete makeover. A second, larger luncheonette was added on the second floor. The entire operation was leased out to Irvin Oster. As he talked to employees upon taking over, he told *What's Cooking?* that the two favorite lunches served at Krauss were liver and onions and red beans and rice.

Red beans and rice is a classic New Orleans dish. It's the embodiment of the term "pot cooking." The dish became associated with Mondays in the city, because Monday was wash day. With the family at home over the weekend, there was no time for mom to do laundry, so it piled up until Monday. The task was an all-day affair in the days before wash-and-wear clothes. With little time for anything else, dinner on Monday had to be something simple and low-maintenance. Red beans and rice was the perfect choice. Mom could put a pot of beans on the stove and let it simmer all afternoon while doing the clothes. If Sunday dinner included a ham or pork roast, the bone went into the bean pot, adding wonderful flavors. When more women entered the workforce, there was no time to even cook red beans at home. Red beans and rice on Mondays evolved from dinner to lunch. It was the simple sort of dish that industrial kitchens such as the one at Krauss could turn out nicely.

There was no signature recipe for red beans and rice at Krauss; the dish varied slightly from year to year, as kitchen staff came and went. Chuck Taggart's recipe on his website, the Gumbo Pages (www.gumbopages.com), is representative of that wash day dinner and the lunches still served across the city on a Monday.

Creole Red Beans and Rice

1 pound dried red kidney beans
1 large onion, chopped
5 ribs celery, chopped
1 bell pepper, chopped
As much garlic as you like, minced (I like lots, 5 or 6 cloves)
1 large smoked ham hock, ¾ pound of Creole-style pickle meat (pickled pork) or ¾ pound smoked ham, diced, for seasoning
1 to 1½ pounds mild or hot smoked sausage or andouille, sliced on the bias
½ to 1 teaspoon dried thyme leaves, crushed
1 or 2 bay leaves
As many dashes Crystal hot sauce or Tabasco as you like, to taste
A few dashes Worcestershire sauce
Creole seasoning blend, to taste; OR,
Red pepper and black pepper to taste
Salt to taste
Rice, cooked
French bread

It's not necessary to soak the beans overnight, but you can if you want to. If you do, drain the water and cover the beans with a double volume of fresh water in the pot. (This helps reduce the, um, flatulence factor.) Bring the beans to a rolling boil. Make sure the beans are always covered by water, or they will discolor and get hard. Boil the beans for about an hour, until the beans are tender but not falling apart.

While the beans are boiling, sauté the Trinity (onions, celery, bell pepper) until the onions turn translucent. Add the garlic and sauté for 2 more minutes, stirring occasionally. After the beans are boiled and drained, add the sautéed vegetables to the beans, then add the ham hock (or ham or pickle meat), smoked sausage, seasonings and just enough water to cover.

Bring to a boil, then reduce heat to a low simmer. Cook for 2 hours at least, preferably 3, until the whole thing gets nice and creamy. Adjust seasonings as you go along. Stir occasionally, making sure that it doesn't burn and/or stick to the bottom of the pot. (If the beans are old—say, older than six months to a year—they won't get creamy. Make sure the beans are reasonably fresh. If it's still not getting creamy, take 1 or 2 cups of beans out and mash them, then return them to the pot and stir.)

Serve generous ladlesful over hot white long-grain rice, with good French bread.

Red beans and rice is usually served with some kind of meat. Sometimes, all a family could afford was the ham that clung to the bone in the pot. Restaurants and cafeterias would serve their beans with smoked or hot sausage, a pork chop or sometimes fried chicken.

Sandwiches and pot cooking continued to be the staples of the Krauss Luncheonette throughout the 1970s and 1980s. The lunch special at Krauss on Tuesday, September 26, 1972, was an "Old-Fashioned Creole Special," consisting of stuffed cabbage, string beans jardinière and corn bread, for ninety-nine cents. Diners who weren't stuffed could add a slice of hot apple pie for dessert for twenty-nine cents. For back-to-school time in 1984, the luncheonette offered a one-dollar hot dog special.

In 1992, Krauss president Hugo Kahn leased the luncheonette to Wayne Baquet Sr. and his wife, Janet. The Baquets operated the family restaurant, Eddie's, on Law Street in Gentilly. Wayne's father, Eddie Baquet Sr., founded the restaurant in 1966, and it was regarded as one of the finest Creole restaurants in the city's history. Baquet also managed the food service operations at Southern University in New Orleans, so he had the

Hugo Kahn (*left*) and Wayne Baquet, sitting at "Eddie's at Krauss" in 1992. *Krauss Collection, University of New Orleans Earl K. Long Library.*

experience to run the employee cafeteria as well as offer the family's classic dishes to shoppers.

When Eddie's at Krauss opened in August 1992, Hugo Kahn was very pleased. He approved an expansion of the luncheonette, adding tables seating twenty-four diners, in addition to the counter that could seat about one hundred. Among the dishes Wayne and Janet Baquet brought to Krauss from the restaurant in Gentilly were fried shrimp stuffed with a crabmeat, the family's classic chicken-andouille gumbo and hot sausage po-boy. Daily specials included red beans and rice, fried seafood plates, burgers and several po-boys: beef brisket, fried shrimp and catfish. Wayne's father, Eddie, who had been retired for a few years, would pop in almost daily to check on the luncheonette, especially the "oyster dressing bread." Wayne explained that this dish started with hollowed-out French bread. The bread was heated

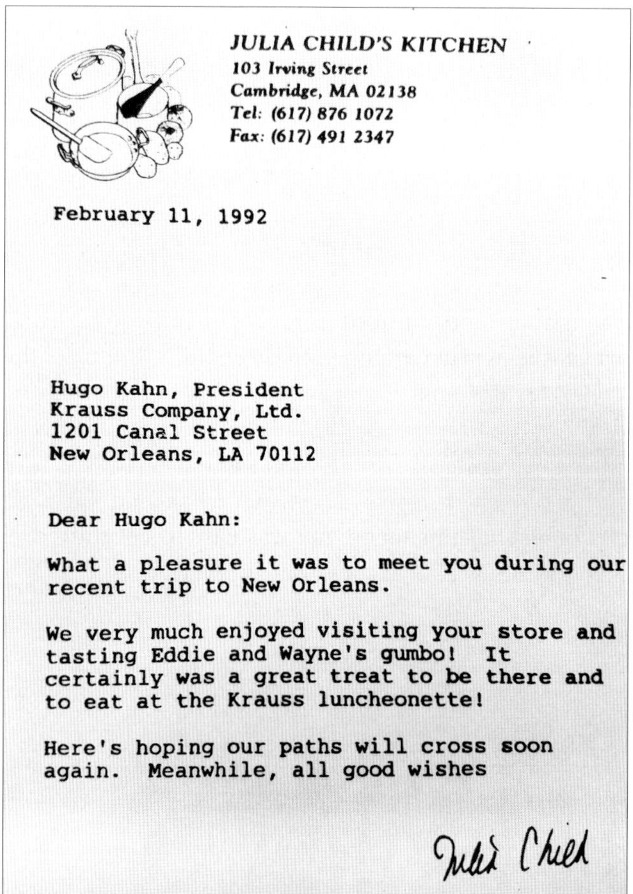

JULIA CHILD'S KITCHEN
103 Irving Street
Cambridge, MA 02138
Tel: (617) 876 1072
Fax: (617) 491 2347

February 11, 1992

Hugo Kahn, President
Krauss Company, Ltd.
1201 Canal Street
New Orleans, LA 70112

Dear Hugo Kahn:

What a pleasure it was to meet you during our recent trip to New Orleans.

We very much enjoyed visiting your store and tasting Eddie and Wayne's gumbo! It certainly was a great treat to be there and to eat at the Krauss luncheonette!

Here's hoping our paths will cross soon again. Meanwhile, all good wishes

Julia Child

Letter from Miss Julia Child to Hugo Kahn, after her visit to the store in 1992. *Krauss Collection, University of New Orleans Earl K. Long Library.*

up with a little butter, filled with oyster dressing and then re-heated. Eddie passed away in 1993 but not before Julia Child visited Krauss in 1992. Child wrote Hugo Kahn on February 11, 1992, complimenting him on "Eddie and Wayne's gumbo."

Eddie's at Krauss also served breakfast, daily, from 10:00 a.m. to 11:00 a.m. The $1.59 breakfast special offered one egg, grits or hash browns, bacon or sausage and a biscuit. Larger breakfast combinations started at $2.99. Lunch was served from 11:00 a.m. until 4:00 p.m.

One month after they opened Eddie's at Krauss, Wayne and Janet opened a new restaurant in Uptown New Orleans. Zachary's, on Oak Street, continued the Baquet family style of cooking. In 1995, Eddie's at Krauss closed. The Baquets chose to focus on Zachary's, which they operated until they sold the restaurant in 2004. The store leased the luncheonette to Chef Ken Mills, who reopened it as the Diner at Krauss. Local food critic and philosopher Tom Fitzmorris gave Chef Ken's food high praise, saying, "Most appealing of all Ken's pot cooking was his crawfish étoufée. It was made with a brown roux and lots of green onions, served uniquely with stuffed crawfish heads. So, really, it was more a bisque than an étoufée, but I may be the only person who ever gave that a second thought."

Unfortunately for Chef Ken, his wizardry in the Diner could not stop the inevitability of Krauss's closure in 1997. He opened another restaurant on Poydras Avenue, eventually leaving New Orleans for Norman, Oklahoma.

Like the figurative neighborhood gumbos that make up New Orleans, real gumbo was a part of the Krauss experience throughout the time the store served lunch. Of all the variations on gumbo served over the years, the Baquet family recipe is the most memorable. Eddie's gumbo was based on a "dry roux." Rather than slowly bringing flour and fat (butter, lard or oil) over a low heat, allowing it to brown on the stove, a dry roux is baked in the oven. Wayne Baquet would explain that this technique was easy to get started in the morning and created a solid level of consistency in the dish.

Fabrics, foundations and food are the three cornerstones of the Krauss legacy.

9

Canal Street Versus Shopping Malls

Feel good music
I've been told
Good for the body
And it's good for your soul
—the Meters, "Hey Pocky A-Way"

New Orleans was an exciting place when Jimmy Heymann asked Hugo Kahn to join the Krauss management team in 1967. The city was already playing a huge role in the space race that John F. Kennedy started when he declared that the United States would put a man on the moon by the end of the decade. On January 9, 1962, the executive assistant to the manager of the Michoud Operations of the George C. Marshall Flight Center, Keith Wible, explained how the city would fit into the race to the moon at a meeting of the Mariners Club of New Orleans. While the club members enjoyed dinner at Kolb's on St. Charles Avenue, Wible explained that the Michoud facility (named because the land in the eastern section of New Orleans was once part of a plantation owned by Antoine Michoud) would be an important component in the production of rocket boosters for the race to the moon. NASA directed Chrysler, Boeing and other contractors to build a massive fabrication plant out there, where big rocket boosters, the Saturn I, Saturn IB and Saturn V, would be built. Louisiana's powerful congressional lobby, particularly Senators Russell Long, Allen Ellender and Representatives F. Edward Hebert and T. Hale Boggs, saw to it that, as the

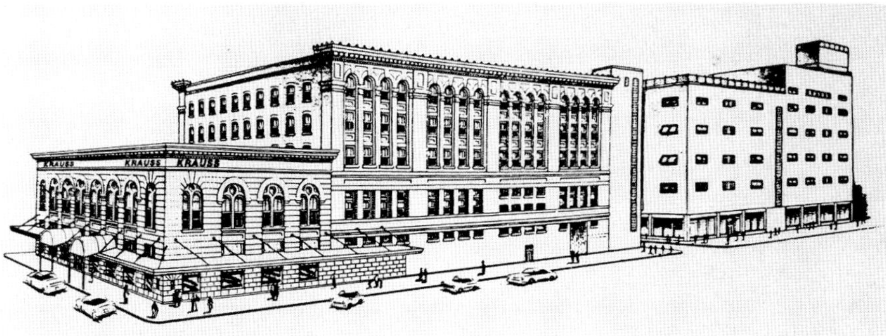

Illustration of Krauss Department Store, from the store's letterhead that was used from 1955 until 1997. *Krauss Collection, University of New Orleans Earl K. Long Library.*

government spent billions to go to the moon, New Orleans would get a piece of the pie. By the end of 1962, two thousand people worked at Michoud. By 1965, almost nine thousand people worked there.

The wide variety of merchandise sold at Krauss was attractive to folks working in well-paying jobs. The after-Christmas sale in 1965 featured deep discounts on Playtex "Living" bras and "Golden Girdles." One of the featured items of the sale were "16 button length" gloves, harkening back to the days of the massive glove department at the Krausz Store on 833 Canal Street in 1897.

The Michoud facility was about fifteen miles to the east of downtown New Orleans. It was natural that homebuilders would construct new subdivisions in the eastern part of Gentilly and across the Industrial Canal. As families moved farther out, so dad could be closer to work, new homeowners turned to Krauss for flooring and carpet. Vinyl "CushionFlor" from Congoleum and "100% Wood Pile Broadloom Carpet" were both for sale in the Linoleum and Carpet Departments on the third floor of the cavernous store at 1201 Canal. Things were happening fast in the late 1960s, and Jimmy Heymann's staff worked hard to keep up. The Fabric Department added fiberglass draperies, "treated with Miracle Teflon," in the fall of 1965, a response to the consumer demand for space age products. The Uniform Department was quite busy as well. Dickies brand "never needs ironing" work clothes were regularly on sale in 1965, as companies desired to put a good foot forward with NASA and the large corporations that subcontracted to them.

Michoud and Gentilly were not the only growth areas in the mid-1960s. Younger New Orleanians looked west to Metairie to build homes

Newspaper ad for mattresses, early 1970s. *Krauss Collection, University of New Orleans Earl K. Long Library.*

of their own. They also needed lamps, housewares, flooring and all the other items that a single trip to Krauss would yield. Delivery service extended throughout the metro area, so those leaving the city for the suburbs could bring Krauss with them.

The economic boom provided by the oil industry and the space race opened up new ventures and opportunities in the city. On November 1, 1966, All Saints' Day, Pete Rozelle, commissioner of the National Football League, held a press conference at the Pontchartrain Hotel, on St. Charles Avenue. Rozelle announced that John Mecom Jr. of Houston, Texas, had been awarded a franchise in the NFL, located in New Orleans. The timing of the announcement was significant; All Saints' Day was a very appropriate day to mark the beginning of the history of the New Orleans Saints football club. New Orleans has a rich Catholic heritage, and many locals pray fervently for deceased family on both All Saints' Day and All Souls' Day, November 2. On September 17, 1967, some 80,700 fans watched as Saint John Gilliam ran back the opening kickoff for a touchdown. The Los Angeles Rams won that first game, but an incredible new aspect of New Orleans culture was born.

Rozelle imposed several conditions on the city and the team's owner when awarding the franchise. The most important was the condition that New Orleans and the state would have to agree to build an enclosed stadium for the team. Rozelle feared that the city's notoriously wet weather would mean home games would be played in a literal swamp. Businessman David Dixon, who spearheaded the movement to bring the NFL to New Orleans, got Governor John McKeithen and Mayor Vic Schiro on board, and the plan to build a domed stadium in New Orleans was launched. While building the stadium in the suburbs was initially considered, the decision was made to place the facility downtown, about ten blocks from Krauss Department Store. After numerous delays, construction of the Superdome began on August 11, 1971. The Saints played their first season in the Superdome in 1975, and the stadium was the site of the Super Bowl in 1978. The construction of the Louisiana Superdome (currently known as the Mercedes-Benz Superdome) led to more jobs for New Orleanians, who then had more money to spend at department stores.

In the fall of 1967, the Uniform and Men's Departments knew that the space race and outdoor construction didn't stop in cold weather, so BVD sweatshirts and long underwear were on sale.

Author Marjorie Arch, who had written two books on sewing, led the Krauss Sewing Clinics in March,1968. The clinics were part of the store's Spring Fabric Fair. Seamstresses could apply their skills to "Paris Imported Couture Fabrics" from Yves Saint Laurent, at $3.98 to $7.98 per yard.

Promotions kept moving in 1968. The store marked its 65th anniversary in April, combining it with the city's 250th anniversary celebrations that spring. Ads in the *Times-Picayune* showed fashions from the store's opening in 1903, as well as enticing shoppers to buy the latest styles.

Jimmy Heymann and Krauss ended the 1960s with a total redesign and renovation of all the ladies' departments on the second floor. The new look included different colors for each department on the floor, as well as new flooring to match. It's interesting that the work was completed by the end of October 1969, which was considered to be well in advance of the holiday shopping season that still officially began after Thanksgiving.

Going into the 1970s, one of the main goals of Krauss Department Store was to continue to offer shoppers interesting reasons to come down to Canal Street. With Maison Blanche operating stores in Metairie and Gentilly and D.H. Holmes and Godchaux's anchoring Lakeside Shopping Center in Metairie, Krauss made sure shoppers were aware of its affordable merchandise, easy credit terms and special programs and presentations. To get teens into the "With-It '70s," the store sponsored a fashion show featuring clothing created from Simplicity Patterns in the Penthouse Cafeteria. Vogue came to Krauss with a similar show in November 1970.

The store brought "Decorama '70" to New Orleans in May 1970. Decorama '70 was a home furnishings and decorating show that traveled the country that year. When Krauss sponsored the show in New Orleans, Betty Price, the store's home fashion coordinator, presented a seminar titled "Mand of California, Carpeting and Decorating Aspects." It was the kind of thing a suburban department store usually didn't have the space to offer. Krauss could invite shoppers up to the auditorium on the sixth floor, offer them a place to eat lunch and spend the day improving their decorating knowledge.

Another approach to appeal to busy shoppers was to go out to their homes to discuss home redecorating. Krauss drapery and slipcover sales consultants would gladly bring samples out to the house, so the stay-at-home-mom could look them over and get professional advice without having to go down to Canal Street.

Five-piece dinette sets were 20 percent off, selling for $79.95, during Community Bargain Days in 1970, and the store was more than happy to deliver. Wash day was much less tedious for the lady of the house in 1970, as wash-and-wear permanent press fashions for men were stylish and affordable. Mail-order service, a longtime Krauss tradition, continued into the days of the suburban mall. Other longtime, practical services, such as shoe repair, attracted workers in office buildings on Canal, as well as the CBD and the Civic Center on Loyola. It was very easy to drop off the items, grab a sandwich at the luncheonette and get back to work, all on a standard lunch hour.

Ludwig Behr, Krauss vice-president for the New York office, passed away on October 23, 1970, at the age of forty-eight. The New York buying office had been a vital part of the store's operation since the early days. The staff there had their fingers on the pulse of the garment district, which enabled them to acquire quality merchandise, particularly discounted lots and surplus inventory.

Krauss kicked off "Old Fashioned Bargain Days" on September 25, 1971, by reprinting the front page of the *Daily Picayune* from Sunday, April 12, 1903. The paper that day announced the grand opening of the store the next day. The luncheonette featured "old-fashioned" daily specials that week in 1971, including Grillades and Gravy over steamed rice with cornbread, for ninety-five cents. The promotion was well received and repeated for several years.

Krauss got its fourth president in the store's history in January 1980, when Jimmy Heymann retired and turned the keys over to Hugo Kahn, the store's vice-president and controller. This marked the first time in its history that control of the store went outside the Krauss-Heymann family. In a full-page advertising feature printed on August 24, 1980, the paper said of Kahn, "If you meet Kahn for the first time, he probably will ask you where you live, whether you shop at Krauss, how often, and if never, why not." Kahn was more than ready for the challenges of continuing the Krauss tradition, with his former boss and friend, Jimmy, staying on as chairman of the board.

The city's "Rediscover Downtown" campaign in 1982 was so successful, it was continued in 1983. Hugo Kahn was able to roll the store's "Discover

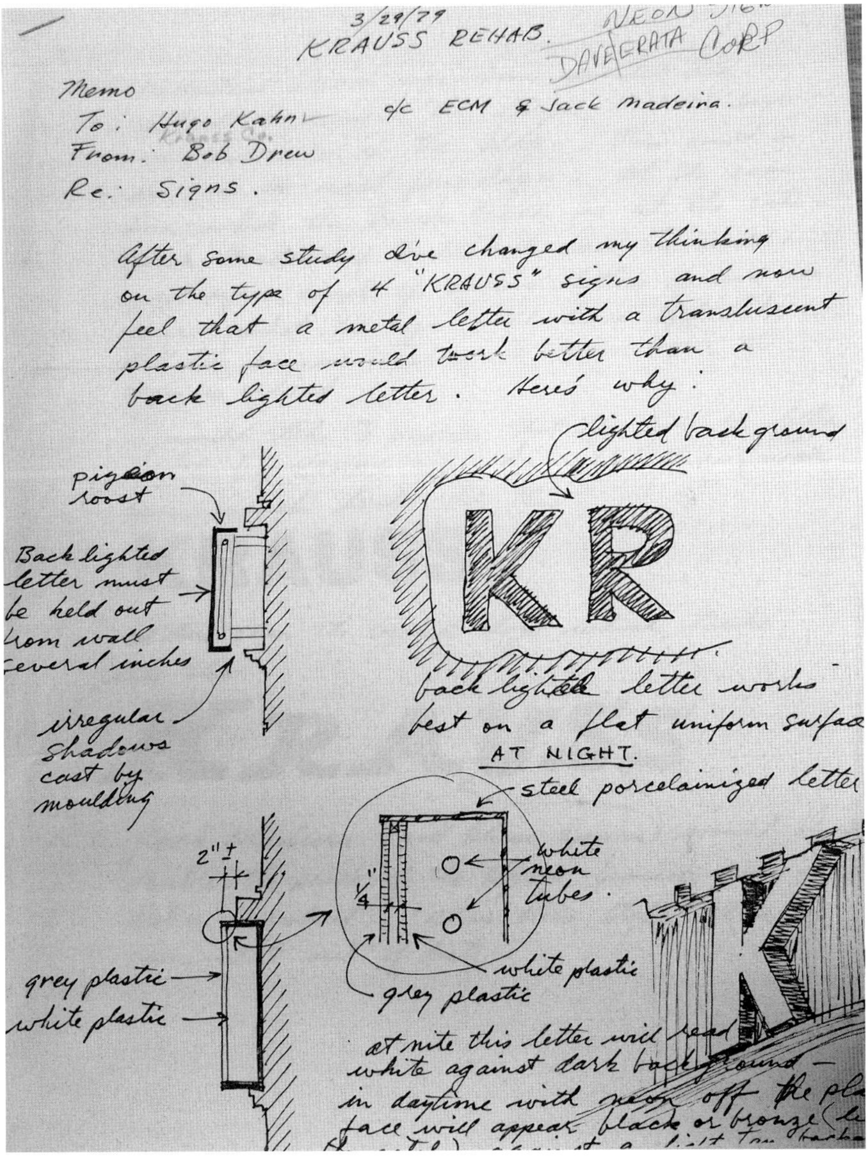
3/29/79
KRAUSS REHAB.
NEON SIGN
DAVE ERATA CORP

Memo
To: Hugo Kahn c/c ECM & Jack Madeira.
Krauss Co.
From: Bob Drew
Re: Signs.

After some study I've changed my thinking on the type of 4 "KRAUSS" signs and now feel that a metal letter with a translucent plastic face would work better than a back lighted letter. Here's why:

at nite this letter will read white against dark background — in daytime with neon off the pla
face will appear black or bronze (

Notes and suggestions on rehabilitating store signs and displays, March 29, 1979. *Krauss Collection, University of New Orleans Earl K. Long Library.*

Krauss" theme that began in 1980 into the larger promotion. In 1983, the store continued emphasizing its sewing seminars and fabric department.

When Ethel Bourgeois began her career at Krauss in 1931, the store had just been air-conditioned. It was a good job for the seventeen-year-old from Mid-City. The *Times-Picayune* profiled Bourgeois in 1982, asking her to reflect on fifty-one years at Krauss. She remembered, "Each morning, my mother gave me 30 cents, 10 cents to ride the streetcar to and from Krauss [5 cents each way], 10 cents to get a good luncheon meal in the employees' cafeteria, like New Orleans red beans and rice with good sausage. And I could use the other 10 cents to buy a soft drink or a snack on my break." It's interesting that the page in the paper that day, November 5, 1982, featured an ad by NOPSI encouraging "Rediscover Downtown" shoppers to take the bus to get to the CBD. In 1982, bus and streetcar fare was sixty cents each way, up 1,100 percent from Ethel's first ride to Krauss in 1931. Offering free ride coupons to shoppers so they could take the bus to the store was a regular feature of Krauss Bargain Days in the mid- to late 1980s.

Krauss Department Store lost Jimmy Heymann on Saturday, March 4, 1985. Heymann, who went from Tulane grad to navy lieutenant before taking over his father's job in 1963, was fondly remembered throughout the community. His son, Jerry Heymann, took over as Chairman of Krauss Co. Inc.

Church Day was another longtime Krauss tradition. The store designated one day in November, before Thanksgiving, where shoppers could designate a church or synagogue, and Krauss would donate 10 percent of their purchase to that institution. In 1985, the State of Louisiana lifted the blue law restrictions that prohibited Krauss and other department stores from opening on Sundays, so the promotion became Church Days that year, on Sunday and Monday, November 24 and 25.

The store's promotions ranged from Church Days to the racetrack. The store sponsored an open house on Sunday, November 21, 1982, at the New Orleans Fair Grounds. The racetrack's grandstand opened to the public at noon. Those who came out to the fair grounds that day were treated to workouts from several of the handicap and stakes horses that would be racing in the season that opened on Thanksgiving Day. The workouts were followed by a performance from the Gretna Mounted Drill Team and their twenty-two palomino horses. There was one exhibition race, a quarter-mile run with three horses ridden by female jockeys. One lucky guest won a raffle for a 1983 Chevrolet Corvette.

Canal Street at night, 1980s (unknown photographer). *Krauss Collection, University of New Orleans Earl K. Long Library.*

Krauss's contribution to the event was a fashion show in the clubhouse. The title of the show was "A Tribute to the Sport of Kings." Krauss fashion director Betty Huddleston provided the commentary for the event. After the show, attendance at which was by invitation-only, guests were entertained by singer Irma Thomas and Dr. Frank Minyard and his band.

The show was a solid success. The title of the 1983 show, held on Sunday, November 20, was "Opening Night." Three of the dresses that

Program for "The Fair Grounds Open House and Krauss' Holiday Fashion Show," November 20, 1983. *Krauss Collection, University of New Orleans Earl K. Long Library.*

came down the runway that evening included a black taffeta from Billy Jack for Her (selling for $48), a black lace dress from McKay for $140 and a black velvet and taffeta dress from Lee Jordan, an upscale item for $252. Notes for the advertising department mentioned that furs would be a main feature of the show and that "big spenders always go for a sure thing!"

Like its competitor, Maison Blanche, Krauss began to hold "warehouse sales" in the 1980s. The Krauss warehouse was located at 1100 South Peters Street, near the Ernest N. Morial Convention Center, along the river. The main feature of the warehouse sales were deep discounts on large appliances, as well as rugs and other home furnishings. Color TVs ranged in price from $300 to $400, and you could buy a VCR at Krauss for $300 in the fall of 1987. If the ladies liked the fashions worn by *Wheel of Fortune* letter-spinner Vanna White, they could shop her collection as well that fall. When the government mandated the breakup of the Bell System in 1982, it was only a matter of time before telephones could be purchased rather than rented. Krauss opened a phone center in the mid-1980s to sell Western Electric phones.

Throughout his time as both president and chairman of Krauss, Jimmy Heymann did not feel the need to expand to the suburbs. He was quite satisfied with the store's performance and profitability on Canal Street. Things had changed in the market by the time Heymann passed away. In 1987, Hugo Kahn and the management team signed a letter of intent with Lakeside Shopping Center and planned to open a Krauss store in Metairie. The plan was for Krauss to take over the southern anchor of the mall, the former location of Godchaux's. The deal for the 70,000-square-foot location fell apart, much to Kahn's disappointment. While other offers for space came in from property owners in Metairie, none of them was for more than 50,000 square feet. Kahn wanted 100,000 to 130,000 square feet for a second Krauss. The status of Lakeside as the premier shopping mall in the metro area was the only exception that would make

Above: Display window on the Basin Street side of Krauss Department Store (photographer unknown). *Krauss Collection, University of New Orleans Earl K. Long Library.*

Left: Cover of the "Krauss Co-Workers Handbook" from the 1980s. *Krauss Collection, University of New Orleans Earl K. Long Library.*

a smaller space acceptable. In the late 1980s, the sales floor made up about half of 1201 Canal Street's 350,000 square feet of space. Of that, about 15,000 square feet was for "piece goods," fabric, thread and such. Kahn was looking for a suburban location that would rival Canal Street.

Keeping good people was also a serious challenge for a store with a single location. Other Canal Street stores had multiple locations, thus offering their managers opportunities for promotion. For example, a sales clerk at one of the local chains could aspire to promotion to assistant manager in their area, such as men's clothing, ladies' shoes, housewares and so on. After some time in that position, the store might call them downtown, offering a position as assistant buyer. That gave them experience with the buying process, as well as more responsibility on the sales floor, as the buyer was often away. The next step after assistant buyer would be a return to the suburbs, as a department or area manager, and possibly then moving into store management.

Krauss didn't have those suburban stores to nurture talent. To that end, the Heymanns, then Kahn had to take steps to keep good people. In a 1988 interview with *New Orleans CityBusiness*, fabrics buyer Jay Klein explained how management at Krauss worked:

> *It's like they're setting you up in business—without the same responsibility. Kahn's strategy was to make Krauss a stable work environment. For buyers, that meant not holding them personally responsible for economic trends. In chain stores, it was easier for executive management to take the attitude, if you can't do the job, we'll fire you and get someone who will. Krauss would recognize factors that were outside of any one individual's ability to control. By not punishing buyers for one bad cycle, they were able to learn and grow in the job. That allowed them to gain valuable experience as well as a desire to stay with Krauss.*

Krauss buyers, along with Hugo Kahn himself, spent more time on the sales floor than top management in most of their competitors. This was a tradition that dated back to the 1930s, when a customer was so pleased with the service he received, he told the department's manager that the salesclerk deserved a raise. That salesclerk was Krauss president Leon Heymann. Unlike the Heymanns, Kahn directly embraced the sales promotions of the late 1980s, wearing T-shirts and sweatshirts that promoted products. Krauss had a "face" in Hugo Kahn it hadn't had before. In the age of aggressive television advertising and color photographs in newspapers, it was necessary for Kahn to be out front and making a connection with the community beyond the boardrooms of local businesses and charitable foundations. Krauss was the store of the average New Orleanian, and Kahn led the way, becoming its chief spokesman and promoter.

10

The End of an Era

Do Whatcha Wanna,
Mardi Gras Morning
—Rebirth Brass Band, "Do Whatcha Wanna"

Krauss Department Store had fought to be profitable in a world of declining downtowns and expanding suburban malls since the 1960s. In 1988, the store faced a unique challenge: a downtown mall. New Orleans Centre opened that year on Poydras Street, right next to the Superdome. It was anchored by Lord & Taylor and Macy's. The mall was part of a trend of businesses leaving Canal Street for Poydras Street. Consolidated Natural Gas Producing Company left One Canal Place with the opening of the office tower next to New Orleans Centre. Texaco had already left 1501 Canal Street, just three blocks from Krauss, for a thirty-two-story skyscraper at 400 Poydras. Other companies followed, shifting the focus away from the city's historic main street.

For decades, the Krauss advertising strategy was simple: daily newspaper ads featuring discounts and other sales, as well as target print ads for specific brands and seasonal goods. In 1988, the store launched a $100,000 television commercial run, targeted at upscale customers.

In general, though, the goal was to get the shopper into the store. Once inside Krauss, the staff knew their massive inventory would do the job from there. A shopper could go into the Sportswear Department and find basics like Levi's jeans, but the more expensive leather jackets were just a few racks away.

Cross-promotion ad, Krauss and the Saenger Theater, 1993. *Krauss Collection, University of New Orleans Earl K. Long Library.*

Downtown shopping took another blow in 1989, when Dillard's acquired D.H. Holmes. The Arkansas-based department store chain closed the Holmes flagship store on Canal Street and continued to operate the suburban stores. Kahn kept up his efforts to find a suitable second suburban location for the store, contacting William Dillard in May 1989 to see if the chain would be interested in disposing of the Holmes location in the Esplanade Mall, located in Kenner, Louisiana, about twelve miles from downtown New Orleans. Dillard replied that his chain would keep that location.

Krauss kept on going, as writers made their way to the store to see the anachronisms, like the pneumatic tube system that linked the sales counters with the office for decades. Since Krauss only had the one store, sales clerks didn't have to call into downtown for approvals on credit purchases. They would ring up the sale on the cash register, put the receipt in the tube, just like a bank customer does at the drive-up. On the office side of the tube, the Credit Department would approve or deny the charge, just like it had done for decades. The big difference in 1990 was that the check of the account was done on a computer terminal.

Canal Street retailers voiced their concerns to city hall, and plans were developed to entice shoppers back. The Downtown Development District (DDD) worked with the New Orleans Regional Transit Authority (NORTA) to create a downtown shuttle bus line. The "Easy Rider" line was a loop that ran down Canal Street from Claiborne Avenue, turned toward Poydras, went up Poydras to the Superdome and backtracked on Claiborne to Canal. The fare was twenty-five cents, and a round-trip took about an hour to make. By the spring of 1990, the line carried around 1,200 riders a day. NORTA and the DDD did an ad campaign suggesting shoppers "park and ride"—parking at the Superdome, then riding the Easy Rider over to Canal Street.

J. Phil Preddy was still working at Krauss in 1990. At the age of ninety, he slowed down a bit, only working twenty hours a week. Still, Krauss

An unknown employee checks sales receipts as Hugo Kahn demonstrates the store's pneumatic tube system in 1989. *Krauss Collection, University of New Orleans Earl K. Long Library.*

Department Store was that important to him that he went down to 1201 Canal Street for a few hours each day. The store's display department was just converting from its "Printasign" machine to personal computers. Unlike many older folks, Preddy didn't see using a computer as an obstacle. He told the *Times-Picayune*, "I learned to work the Printasign about 20 years ago, and before that they had a machine that was old when I got here." Preddy passed away in February 1995. At his funeral, he was praised and loved by family, friends and co-workers.

Other longtime employees were still going strong in 1990. Rosemary Dauterive started at the store in 1953, working at the new luncheonette. After seventeen years on the second floor, she moved to gift wrap. Eventually, she managed a combined department that gift-wrapped packages for in-store customers and handled packaging for delivery and mail order. She described the shift from food service to gift wrap as a challenge, but by 1990, Dauterive was happy, to the point where she said she would work part-time after retiring.

Rosemary Dauterive started at Krauss behind the luncheonette counter in 1953 and retired as the gift wrap/shipping manager in 1993. *Krauss Collection, University of New Orleans Earl K. Long Library*.

Krauss was a family that loved, hated, laughed and cried together. The staff also solved crises for customers regularly. In the summer of 1991, Bethany Bourgeois, from the suburban city of Gretna, Louisiana, competed in the Miss Louisiana Pre-Teen pageant. Her mother, Jennifer, told the story of the day of the pageant in a letter to the president of Krauss, which naturally went straight to Hugo Kahn. When mother and daughter arrived at the Clarion Hotel on Canal Street for the competition, they learned that the formal dress Bethany was to wear was supposed to be floor-length, but the dress she had was tea-length. Jennifer immediately took her daughter to Krauss, in the hopes of finding a floor-length dress. They found something just as good—lace in the fabric department that matched Bethany's dress, giving it the additional four inches of length it needed. Crisis averted!

Even though Hugo Kahn was now the father of the Krauss Department Store family, the Heymanns were still part of that number. Krauss chairman of the board Jerry Heymann came down from his home in New York for various local events, such as a fundraising dinner in January 1991 for Southern Repertory Theater at Antoine's Restaurant. His mother, Johnnie

Bethany Bourgeous, Miss American Pre-Teen contestant, with an unidentified clerk in the Fabric Department, summer 1991. *Krauss Collection, University of New Orleans Earl K. Long Library.*

Heymann, had recently moved from the family's Audubon Place home to a penthouse in the One River Place condominium development, located at Poydras Street and the river.

The Krauss staff regularly received praise from shoppers. On June 22, 1992, Claire P. Moledour mailed a note to "To Whom It May Concern" at Krauss. She said, "I would like to compliment Krauss on their courteous and helpful employees! Any time I have shopped in your store, I have been impressed by their pleasant attitudes and treatment of your customers." All of these sorts of letters and notes made their way to Hugo Kahn. A secretary would open the mail and check to see if the correspondent had a Krauss charge account. The letters, with the additional data, were sent to Kahn, who regularly sent back written responses.

Canal 2000 was the name of the Canal Street merchants and property owners' association created in February 1992. The goal of the association was to work with leasing agents to lure national store chains to Canal. The merchants and property owners planned to work up incentives and leasing guidelines, in the hopes that a show of unity would attract serious tenants.

Dr. Torrey Wilson, a New Orleans native who became a psychiatrist and now lived in Chicago, regularly told his father, Luther, that he should retire. Even though he was sixty-two, Luther Wilson still parked cars at the Krauss garage six days a week. Wilson explained that it wasn't so much about his skill at parking cars (which was excellent) as his ability to remember which car belonged to which customer. Regular shoppers at Krauss, including New Orleans music icon Irma Thomas, trusted Wilson with her car on her weekly trips to the store. Even though the store wasn't as busy as it used to be in the heyday of Canal Street shopping, Wilson still kept up with the cars. His five sons all worked with him at one time or another when they were growing up. Unlike Luther, all seven of the Wilsons graduated from high school, and several of them had gone on to college.

Sales were up during the 1993 holiday season, particularly jewelry and watches. Hugo Kahn boasted to the *Times-Picayune* on December 3, 1993, that his store had just sold a $3,000 dining set.

Sales were up, but shopping styles had changed dramatically over the years on Canal Street. In a 1994 profile, longtime Hat Department manager Flo Ferguson considered a hat an essential for ladies going shopping. "You wouldn't dare go to Canal Street without one. You wore stockings, you wore heels, you wore gloves and you wore a hat. It was a must." Krauss was still the place to go and Ferguson the lady to see if you wanted a good hat. Twice a year, since the 1960s, hat designer Jack McConnell would come to New Orleans, specifically to Krauss. McConnell's hats sold for $250 or more, but Ferguson had no problem providing him with buyers. Flo Ferguson was seventy-four in 1996 and had absolutely no intention to retire.

Eddie Bronston "retired" from Krauss in 1974. That is to say, he gave up the title and salary of executive vice-president of Krauss Company, Inc. Twenty years later, Bronston still found himself going to 1201 Canal Street six days a week, from 9:00 a.m. to about 3:00 p.m. All those years working in the furniture department, as a sales clerk and a department's buyer before moving into store management, gave him a perspective the store still appreciated in 1994. As much as Bronston enjoyed playing cards in the legendary Ghost Club game at the Fairmont Hotel, the legalized gambling that had come to New Orleans in the 1990s didn't impress him. Still, at eighty-nine, Bronston was going strong. He told *Times-Picayune* reporter David Cuthbert, "There are a couple of things that really matter in life. One's family, and the other is work. Find something you like, something that interests you, and work at it."

Several Orleans Parish Public Schools joined the trend of adopting uniforms for students in the mid-1990s. One of the companies offering uniforms was a local business, Classic Kids Heritage Uniforms. Its clothing was styled after Kente cloth, brightly colored patterns originating in the historical Ashanti kingdom of West Africa. When designers Tammy Martin and Desiree Edwards pitched their designs to public and Catholic schools in the city, they were well received. Martin and Edwards connected with a manufacturer in Eunice, Louisiana, and Krauss carried the uniforms for schools such as Oretha Castle Haley Elementary and Bishop Perry Middle School, a Catholic school that closed after Hurricane Katrina.

Like many urban areas, gun violence plagued New Orleans in the mid-1990s. In 1995, one of the attempts to get guns off the streets was Operation Hope. In exchange for bringing in a gun, donors would receive gift certificates from sponsoring stores, bags of groceries from local supermarkets or one of several hundred sewing machines donated by Krauss.

On July 15, 1996, after forty-seven years at the store, Vera Helmers retired from Krauss. She was the head of the Sales Audit Department. She still planned to come in two days a week to check up on her department, though. It's what Krauss folks did.

Throughout the history of Krauss, the company's real estate acquisitions did not face much scrutiny. The Storyville neighborhood was not considered important, and when the red-light district was razed and the area turned into a public housing project, it became even less historically significant. There were a few buildings behind the store and along Basin Street that remained by the 1990s, and two of them were owned by Krauss. In 1996, Krauss demolished a triplex located in the 1200 block of Bienville Street, directly behind the Krauss service building. There was debate over the historic significance of the building. Built around 1855, the building at 1208–12 Bienville had been in the family of Robert Maestri, mayor of the city in the 1930s. During the Storyville period, the building contained several cribs, rooms used by prostitutes who did not work at the higher-level sporting clubs along Basin Street. The city considered designating the building as a landmark, but the designation was not granted. The building was in such bad shape by 1996 that it had to be demolished. Krauss still owned the building that Leon Fellman bought from Lulu White in the 1920s. That building, on the corner of Bienville and Basin, had gone from being a saloon to a small grocery store.

One advantage Krauss held over many of its competitors over the years was its ability to operate successfully with a small profit margin. The privately

Kathy Trosclair Lapeyrouse with her mother, Mrs. Richard J. Trosclair, pose outside the store on their last visit to Krauss, September 1, 1997. *Krauss Collection, University of New Orleans Earl K. Long Library.*

held corporation was answerable to the Heymann family, not a group of shareholders. The store took a large loss in sales in 1996, and things did not look any better for 1997. Kahn and the owners consulted and decided the store should close while it could meet its obligations, rather than be forced into bankruptcy. When the plan to close was made public in July 1997, the outpouring from the community was overwhelming. By the summer of 1997, there were about 230 employees at the store, a number much lower than the labor-intensive 1950s and 1960s. They would be laid off—but in time to hopefully find other jobs before the Christmas rush. As Kahn would explain, over and over, "The arithmetic doesn't work anymore."

The eulogies from writers near and far appeared in the papers and magazines. With ninety-three years of memories, so many people came by for their last opportunities to shop at the store, eat at the luncheonette and enjoy a bit of New Orleans that was fading. One of the groups taking that last trip to Krauss was the New Orleans City Council. On September 4, 1997, after passing a resolution commending the store for ninety-four years of service to New Orleans, Councilmembers Suzanne Terrell, Ellen Hazeur-Distance, Jim Singleton and Roy Glapion all walked over from city hall to the Diner at Krauss for one last lunch.

On September 5, 1997, Stacie Riley, class president of room 129 at Ernest Morial Elementary, in New Orleans East, wrote Mr. Kahn to thank him for donating an air conditioner for their classroom. "Even though we have a ceiling fan and our teacher, Mrs. Jackson, lets us bring our frozen bottles of water each day, it was still very hot," Stacie wrote. Krauss fixed that for the kids, creating what would be a new generation of Krauss customers, if only the store could keep going.

GENERAL TIMETABLE

Tues., July 29, 1997	* Sign package arrives at the store.
	* Strapping tape and "All Sales Final" stamps arrive at the store.
	* Store closing meeting with store management
	* After close of business, signs should be displayed in the manner prescribed by the Mickey Shelton.
	* Development of payroll budgets, and delivery fee schedule.
	* GOB license should be obtained.
Thur., July 31, 1997	* The liquidation sale event begins. We will be offering discounts of 10% off Electronics, Appliances. All other merchandise in the store will receive a 20% discount.
	* The first ad will be run in the paper.
Thur., Aug. 14, 1997	* Double marking and taping should be complete.
Wed., Aug. 20, 1997	* Warehouse should be emptied into store, or warehouse sale will commence.
Approx. 10 to 12 weeks after sale start date.	* Store will be closed, and left in a broom clean condition.

Timetable for the closing of Krauss Department Store, summer–fall 1997. *Krauss Collection, University of New Orleans Earl K. Long Library.*

Schottenstein Bernstein Capital Group LLC of Columbus, Ohio, laid out a general plan for the store's closing. Liquidation sale advertisements ran in the newspaper at the beginning of August. The Worker Adjustment and Retraining Notification Act (WARN Act) notices went out to federal and state officials, as well as Mayor Marc Morial, on October 23, 1997. Those notifications stated that the store's last day would be Saturday, October 25, 1997. Shoppers flooded the store to scoop up the deeply discounted merchandise that remained. Current and former employees visited with longtime customers, everyone making the best of a sad occasion. Hugo Kahn walked the sales floor, chatting with everyone. Cathy Carmack, daughter of millinery manager Flo Ferguson, brought a video camera to work that day, to capture the memories. Kathy Trosclair Lapeyrouse came up from Houma, Louisiana, to say goodbye to Mister Hugo. She posed for photos with Kahn in his office, and one final photo outside the store with her mother.

By 7:00 p.m., Krauss Department Store was, as Benny Grunch would sing later, "Ain't Dere No More."

A skeleton crew continued to work at 1201 Canal Street, as Krauss liquidated display cases, furniture and other items. By February 1998, the first floor was emptied and was the location of the big post-parade party for

Bargain hunters at Krauss's closing sale, October 25, 1997. *Krauss Collection, University of New Orleans Earl K. Long Library.*

Hugo Kahn (*rear, center*) and the final-day closing crew pose for one last photo on the first floor, October 25, 1997. *Krauss Collection, University of New Orleans Earl K. Long Library.*

the Krewe du Vieux. The irreverent Carnival organization paraded the usual route, from Franklin Avenue and Royal Street in the Bywater neighborhood, heading up into the French Quarter, emerging on North Rampart Street, ending at the party.

Hugo Kahn was still at work in his fifth-floor office in 1998, as speculation ran across New Orleans about what would become of the Krauss store. Some thought it would become a big box store, like Walmart. Others hoped it would be suitable for some other purpose. Kahn remained the public face of Krauss. Several developers approached the company with proposals. In 2001, a deal was close to reality. The development would keep the original two-story portion of the building. The remainder of the store would be demolished, and a high-rise hotel would be built on the site. The September 11, 2001 attacks complicated the developer's ability to close the deal, and it fell through.

Kahn received the Weiss Award by the National Conference for Community and Justice in November 2000. His service to the city, most notably with Canal 2000, the Central Business District Historical Landmarks

NORTA streetcar 2005 passes in front of the 1201 Canal Street Condominiums, October 10, 2016. *Author photo.*

Commission, Tikvat Shalom Congregation and the Jewish Federation of New Orleans, made the award as well deserved as when Leon Fellman received it.

In 2004, condominium developer Elie Khoury made an offer on the Krauss building. The plan he presented to the public called for converting the store and warehouse into 250 condominiums. Khoury expected the units to sell between $149,000 and $249,000. Hurricane Katrina and its aftermath delayed the project until 2009. The 1201 Canal Condominiums are an exciting part of downtown New Orleans, giving folks a chance to "own a piece of New Orleans History."

Krauss Department Store was an important part of the city of New Orleans for ninety-four years of the twentieth century. Former employees and shoppers still walk by the building, thinking back on fond memories of work and life in the Crescent City.

Bibliography

Branley, Edward J. *Maison Blanche Department Store*. Charleston, SC: Arcadia Publishing, 2010.

———. *New Orleans: The Canal Streetcar Line*. Charleston, SC: Arcadia Publishing, 2004.

Chase, John. *Frenchmen, Desire, Good Children and Other Streets in New Orleans*. Rev. ed. New Orleans, LA: Pelican Publishing, 2001.

Higgins, Earl. *The Joy of Y'at Catholicism*. New Orleans, LA: Pelican Publishing, 2007.

Krauss Collection, Louisiana and Special Collections, Earl K. Long Library, University of New Orleans, 2017.

Laborde, Peggy Scott and John Magil. *Canal Street, New Orleans' Great Wide Way*. New Orleans, LA: Pelican Publishing, 2006.

Lind, Angus. *Prime Angus: Readers' Favorite Columns Reprinted From the Pages of The Times-Picayune*. New Orleans, LA: Arthur Hardy Enterprises, 2009.

McCusker, John. *Creole Trombone: Kid Ory and the Early Years of Jazz*. Oxford: University of Mississippi Press, 2013.

Toledano, Roulhac, and Mary Louise Christovich. *New Orleans Architecture: Faubourg Tremé and the Bayou Road (New Orleans Architecture Series, Book 6)*. New Orleans, LA: Pelican Publishing, 2003.

Widmer, Mary Lou. *New Orleans in the 1920s*. New Orleans, LA: Pelican Publishing, 1993.

Index

U

V

W

About the Author

New Orleans native Edward J. Branley is a former high school history teacher. He has written five books for Arcadia Publishing, including *Legendary Locals of New Orleans* and Images of America books *New Orleans: The Canal Streetcar Line*, *Maison Blanche Department Store* and *New Orleans Jazz*. He is graduate of Brother Martin High School in New Orleans and the University of New Orleans.